César

PIERRE RESTANY

TRANSLATED BY JOHN SHEPLEY

HARRY N. ABRAMS, INC., PUBLISHERS, NEW YORK

Illustrations and documents assembled and supplied by Denyse Durand-Ruel

Layout by Peter Knapp and Walter Rospert

Library of Congress Cataloging in Publication Data

Restany, Pierre.
    César.

    Bibliography: p.
    Includes index.
    1. Baldaccini, César, 1921-   I. Title.
NB553.B22R4713   730'.92'4   74-30064
ISBN 0-8109-0358-X

Library of Congress Catalogue Card Number: 74-30064
© Copyright 1975 in Monaco by Éditions André Sauret, Monte-Carlo
Published 1976 by Harry N. Abrams, Incorporated, New York
All rights reserved. No part of the contents of this book may be
reproduced without the written permission of the publishers

Printed and bound in France

Contents

List of Illustrations

Colorplates are marked with an asterisk (*)

César by Pierre Restany

The good fortune of the twentieth century will be seen to lie in its sculpture. The major advances in metal sculpture in the wake of such pioneers as Pablo Gargallo and Julio González; the artistic baptism of the industrial object, which began with Marcel Duchamp's idea of the Ready-made, and the extraordinary experimentation with the object that has been the result; the infinite prospects opened up by the encounter between art and technology; Kinetic Art; Environments and Happenings; the differing concepts of the organization of space; and the direct manipulation of natural ecological elements—these chief landmarks in the development of contemporary art have helped to shape the course of sculpture through the evolution of the very idea of art. One cannot speak of a great modern sculptor such as César without taking note of this structural change in our sensibility.

Contrary to what one might conclude from certain of its high points—Cézanne, Matisse, Braque, Malevich, Mondrian, Klee, Max Ernst, Dali, Jean Fautrier, Wols, Jackson Pollock, Mark Rothko, Kandinsky—painting has not been the determining catalyst in the development of the sensibility of our age. Quite the contrary. Twentieth-century painting, like a superb display of fireworks, has assumed in almost every sense the romantic, sentimental, and pseudomodernist outlook of the last century; it has closed all the doors and blocked all exits from the poetic two-dimensional world. Cézanne prefigured Cubism, of which Braque was the ingenious but limited artisan; Matisse exhausted the resources of color, Klee those of ephemeral fantasy; Kandinsky pursued the vicious circle of nonrepresentation; Mondrian and Malevich were prophets of a modern Constructivist theory whose actual results have led to the multidimensional and technological transfer of basic equations: the simple forms and the pure colors have become light and movement. The unnatural union of painting and literature constituted the romantic epidemic of the century: the Surrealism of André Breton masks under a libertarian and fantastic disguise the most anachronistic fetishism of sentiment.

Beyond the *art informel* of a Fautrier or the *tachisme* of a Wols, Action Painting marks the extreme limits of the artist's independence in expressing his emotionality: Pollock's dripped paintings illustrate in a manner as sublime as it is pathetic the self-annihilating result of the revolt by gesture, the fatal exhaustion of an idiom that has willingly become identified with physical gesture. On the other hand, the fascinating perspectives of pure contemplation evolved by Rothko have led to the conformist and decorative impasse of color-field painting and post-painterly abstraction which the "cool" style of the 1970s readily adopted.

The myth of Picasso's supervitality dominates our era only to enclose it, or rather to drive it back into anachronism and academicism. Time will perhaps one day allow us to judge the Picasso phenomenon in its proper perspective and to see him primarily as one of the pioneers of twentieth-century sculpture. The admiration and respect accorded him by contemporary sculptors, led by César, is highly significant and is directed toward his Cubist collages, his assemblages of the 1930s, and some of his later sheet-iron cutouts.

In truth, the sensibility of the twentieth century was born with the advent of a specific instinct for modernity, that is to say, with a new sense—urban, industrial, and public—of nature. As we entered the age of the image and the mass media, and as our eyes were saturated by film, television, comic strips, and posters, the importance of traditional pictorial iconography gradually became increasingly rarefied along with a continuous diminution of its psychosensorial impact. This is explained by the concurrent situation of painting in relation to the visual mass media, which are today perfectly rational and effective. Political commitment does nothing to compensate for the significant attrition of pictorial art. We know what has become of Social Realism. The "New Figuration" in Europe, a pale subproduct of American Pop Art, is poorly equipped to resist the competition of comic strips and wall posters. If traditional iconography is to retain a place in our visual world, it must play the game of the mass media and fight information techniques on their own ground. And in fact the only present iconographic renewal is resolutely extra-pictorial: Mec Art (or Mechanical Art), which has recourse exclusively to photomechanical means—such as transfers, photoengraving techniques, and enlargements of negatives on emulsified surfaces—in order to restructure the flat image and totally objectify it. Inspired by the same sense of competition, the movements grouped under the label of Hyperrealism tend to render the shock effect of the photographic snapshot by combining decalcomania and coloring by *pochoir* stencils—a sorry compromise, understandable in terms of sentiment but scarcely effective at the level of visual communication.

The significant decline of pictorial art is not due solely to the saturation of the eye in a competitive technical climate. The modern visual world has profoundly changed our sensitivity to the environment. Contemporary sculpture, by assimilating the latest developments of technology, naturally takes full account of the reality of urban and technical folklore, a direct product of our consciousness of modern life. The sculptor, for whom quantity is the true measure of things, is integrated, naturally, with his industrial surroundings. After World War II, metal sculpture passed from the period of the amateur blacksmith to that of the expert welder—from tinkering to more sophisticated industrial techniques. The artists who carried out this transition and who embodied it in their work have thereby identified themselves with the collective sensibility of their time. In this light, César's example takes on the importance of true testimony. The industrialization of sculpture has accelerated the developments in the areas of movement, sound, and light (mechanical, electronic, audio-visual animation). In quick reaction to the analytical and overly mental approaches of the pictorial idiom, industrial sculpture has provided us with the occasion for a change in our psychosensorial attitudes in relation to the object. Above all, by releasing in us an intuitive sense of the communication potential of space, it has made us rediscover individually a sense of space and the need to organize it. The "objects" of modern industrial sculpture have forced us to emerge from ourselves by overturning our conformist habits of seeing, feeling, and thinking. The sculptural object, by becoming a space-time "event," has obliged us to exercise a synthesizing and total vision. This is a salutary exercise that unleashes the creative ego and stimulates us to act directly on nature, exalting the values of active perception, autonomy of the self, and of behavior as a work of art—in a word, the underlying values of a language of direct communication. If the sculptor has been able to profit by the immense scientific progress of the postwar period, if he has integrated himself into the technological universe of the Second Industrial Revolution, it is because he was more qualified than anyone else to do so, subject as he has always been to the Heraclitean law of conflict: conflict between space and material, between inertia and movement, between form and the formless. Technology, by giving him a hitherto unequaled power over his material, has swayed his craftsman's sensibility in the realm of behavior. For the first time, man the "maker" became man the "doer"—the demiurge transformed into a man of action, thereby responsible for his deeds. Technology contributes a new dimension to the sensibility of the artist, that of prescience, of the programming and control of the work process. The idea becomes inseparable from the object. This particular virtue of art—the consideration of sculpture as an object-idea—has opened the way to a more radical concept of aesthetics, in particular, to a series of measures, implemented since 1967, that attempt to make explicit the mechanism, progress, and process of the idea (Process Art). It is interesting to note in this context the "conceptual" development of such Minimalist sculptors as Sol Lewitt, Carl André, and Robert Morris.

The painter—the willing victim of his fetishistic attachment to traditional means and, above all, the possessor of an often unrealistic, cerebral, and sentimental imagination—has of necessity only been able to establish his superior position in the midst of worldwide change. Despite the return to favor—after 1972—of an extremely provincial, photographically realistic style of painting, figurative painting as a whole has tried in vain to stake out for itself a private domain in the visual world of our technical civilization of the image. Lyrical abstract painting (Abstract Expressionism in America, or *art informel* in Europe) has identified itself with the denial of reality —it has become an art of escape to the world of pure individual emotion. In this sense, it constitutes one of the end results of the pessimistic Romanticism of the last century, of the negative attitude toward technical progress connected with the first Industrial Revolution and man's lack of preparation for it, of the proletarianization of the masses and the alienation of the individual conscience. Distrust of the machine as the devourer of men engendered the myth of a universal apocalypse through mechanical excess. Today, in the midst of the Second Industrial Revolution—that of atomic energy, electronics, and interplanetary navigation—our attitude in the face of accelerating technology is one of reasoned optimism. The more science progresses, the more we realize that it is necessary for man to be at the center of everything. If this were not true, if this fundamental humanistic value were not implicitly recognized, the scientist would lose his right to imagination. The present great technological powers have chosen—highly significantly—not to mythologize the conquest of space, not to make the astronauts supermen or conquistadors, but the bearers of humanity's mission in new biochemical and geophysical environments. Gagarin and Armstrong are explorers whose precisely programmed actions were coordinated and sustained by the work of a large team of specialists, a true collective of operational research.

Certainly, recent history has opened our eyes to the dangers of irresponsible science and to the practical abuses of technology. But we also know that technology contains within itself the remedies for its own evils and its own abuses. The widespread campaigns all over the world against air and water pollution underline the misdeeds of an abusive technology, but testify indirectly to modern man's faith in a science that redeems these very abuses.

The true precursors of twentieth-century modernity were the Futurists, who aimed at a total sensibility linked to speed, to industry, to a new manner of living—a new life style. But, unfortunately, the Futurists were provincial Italians who had felt the need to go abroad to formulate their credo and who, after having excited Europe and especially Russia, allowed themselves to be caught up by the "*bonne peinture*" of the Paris Cubists. It is better not to speak of their unfortunate return to their native country. Among them, only Umberto Boccioni—because he was essentially a great sculptor—might possibly have been able to avoid the trap of aesthetic formalism. His premature death in 1916 leaves the question forever unanswered.

The Dadaists took up, in part, the positive achievements of the Futurists—notably their collective excesses, totally nihilistic in appearance. Kurt Schwitters, with his collages, his Merzbau and Merztheater, and his phonetic poems, went further in his work than any follower of Marinetti.

But credit for making the first leap must go to Marcel Duchamp. His Ready-mades (such as the bicycle wheel, bottle rack, and urinal) are mass-produced industrial objects promoted to the rank of sculpture simply by the choice of their "inventor." On what is this aesthetic baptism of the ordinary object based? On the moral conscience of the artist, who assumes responsibility for the choice. In so doing, he shows us the object in a new light; acting completely as an artist, he sets it before us as a work of art.

Duchamp's gesture was essential for the formation of the contemporary sensibility. By switching aesthetics with ethics, art with morality, he overturned the hierarchy of the psychosensorial values of creation and transferred the problem from the design of the work to that of behavior. It was this transfer of artistic sensibility that his contemporaries refused to acknowledge, preferring, under cover of his detached and acquiescent silence, to consider the Ready-mades as the point of no return of non-art. When one remembers that the first Ready-mades (1913–14) are exactly contemporary with the Cubist collages (in particular, Picasso's famous *Still Life*), one can measure the importance of this change in creative thought.

Nevertheless, it required more than forty years for the lesson of Duchamp to be finally understood, and for the problem of the appropriation of the object to be taken up again where he had left it. These forty years coincide with the liquidation of Dada by Surrealism and the development of a nonfigurative pictorial ideology. The reaction against the "abstractionization" of the artistic sensibility was carried out by American Neo-Dadaists and European New Realists between 1955 and 1962. By inserting found objects (Ready-mades) into an Abstract Expressionist pictorial context, Robert Rauschenberg marked the irreversible decline of Action Painting, but, at the same time, he stressed the expressive possibilities of the folklore of our modern technological society. His Combine Paintings opened the way to Pop Art, whose leaders, beginning with Andy Warhol, systematically utilized all the elements of this folklore. Warhol, who had recourse to industrial photographic processes, initiated a photomechanical restructuring of the flat image and a ready-made, extrapictorial iconography.

Yves Klein rediscovered the moral position of Duchamp through the mystical means of cosmogenesis. Transcending the Suprematism of Malevich, and Rothko's "walls of light"—Constructivism and contemplation—Klein concentrated on monochromy and the immaterial, on the tangible perception of the cosmic energy that freely circulates in space and is the basis for all emotive communication. By appropriating this "filled void," Klein was able to act on the sensibilities of others. From this concept derives the fundamental characteristic of European New Realism—the appropriation of the real by means of its parts—that would lead Arman to make his *Accumulations*; Raymond Hains and Mimmo Rotella, their décollages; Tinguely, the kinetic animations made of scrap-iron; Daniel Spoerri, his "trap paintings"; Christo, his "wrappings"; and—last but not least—would influence César to create his automobile *Compressions*.

César finds himself exactly at the juncture of a recent tradition of craftsmanship—metal sculpture—and of a new sense of modern society. This position makes him a phenomenon at once fascinating, complex, and, for certain superficial observers, disconcerting. He is a master of welded metal who effects a transformation of the material in the *Compressions*; a colossus of the " Imprint"; a magician with plastic who has become the first monumental sculptor in that medium; a refined artisan and reckless seeker who cuts up paper, burns matchboxes, crushes toys and jewelry, and treats molten glass like polyester resin. His artistic gifts—mastery of his craft, combined with an exceptional feel for the material, a remarkably acute vision, and a true poetic flair—make César a shaper of the creative sensibility of today, one of our most masterful demiurges of the visual, and one of the greatest artists of all times.

Such a torrent of praise is not gratuitous on my part. It is the result of a lengthy analysis of the causes of the radical change in contemporary sensibility and the consequent evolution of the idea of art. César the man, poet of the visual, artisan and experimental seeker, has been, from the first, at the heart of the situation. Despite hesitations and doubts—but faultlessly and unerringly once the choice was made—he has been able to master *completely* a given sector of the shifting expressivity of contemporary visual language. The study of a particular case like César's is indispensable for an understanding of present-day art, its possibilities and limits, its logic and contradictions, and finally its potential for further development.

15

Continued on page 17

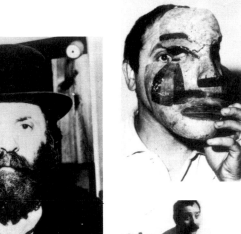

First of all, who is César the man? The person is as diverse as his work, and in appearance infinitely more contradictory. He is the victim of gossip columnists and scandal sheets, and even today, at the height of his fame, he leaves a great many critics perplexed. Their mistake lies in trying to confine César to one category or another, whether it be one of judgment, of style, or of society. He must be accepted as he is—always himself—in all his many aspects. Michel Ragon, who organized the French exhibition at the São Paulo Bienal in 1967 and made César's work the focus of his selection, summed him up as follows: "What a complex figure is this artist, who... is now figurative, now abstract, and sometimes on the same day, who joins a group only to part company with it, and seems merely... to follow his own caprice, his own inclination, sometimes indulging in humorous banter, then recovering himself in a tone of unexpected gravity. An exuberant Southerner whose clowning masks perpetual anxiety, an enthusiast who is prey to the phantoms his own tools have created, an insolent artist who dares to exhibit compressed vehicles as though they were his own work, but who at the same time is capable, when he likes, of such perfection that he has been called the 'Benvenuto Cellini of scrap-iron.'"[1] It can all be reduced, as I have said many times, to a fundamental duality in César between the *homo faber*, the loving and exacting master of his material, and the *homo ludens*, the dazzled poet of modern society, subject to all its entreaties, the visionary seeker whose gaze is forever new. With César anguish precedes choice. Once the decision is made, the artist affirms his sureness of instinct and sense of responsibility. From then on, there is nothing illogical in César speaking simultaneously like Rodin and Duchamp. This is, moreover, the measure of his true stature.

The ambiguities of his social nature derive from the fact that in less than two years César passed almost with no transition from the stage of a late student and the precarious existence of a jack-of-all-trades to that of a Paris celebrity. It was between 1954 and 1956 that this sudden leap forward took place. He was then thirty-three years old, and, since his birth, had probably seen every sort of misfortune.

César Baldaccini was born of Italian parents on January 1, 1921, in the Belle de Mai quarter of Marseilles. It is easy to imagine what life must have been like for young César, son of a cooper turned bistro-keeper, in the sordid, chaotic immigrant neighborhood where his family lived. Even today the Mediterranean sun cannot dispel the extreme sadness of this depressed area. There were some inhabitants who gave the quarter its character, and César has countless anecdotes about them: the uncle, the aunt, the depraved little girl cousin, the "assimilated" immigrant who made an effort to speak with a correct accent. César, himself, has retained the characteristic accent and pure phonetic sound of the original Tuscan dialect of his ancestors, although he does not speak it especially well.

He attended the municipal school until the age of twelve, learning to read and—barely—to write. He then worked with his father in the bistro in the rue Loubon. In 1935, he began evening courses at the École des Beaux-Arts in Marseilles, where he studied modeling and drawing. From there he entered Cornu's studio. He recalls his first teacher: "My professor had been a quarrier, he had cut stone for Rodin... his hands were five times as big as mine. He had great human qualities. He never talked to us about art, only about craft." In this evocation of the past, part of a statement that appeared in a Paris weekly (*Le Nouvel Observateur*, 27 January 1969), the artist's basic dualism is apparent: on the one hand "craft," the technical mastery of the material; on the other "art," the surrender to the poetic quest, to life. Art is life, with all its beauty and contradictions.

In 1943, César passed the entrance examination for the École des Beaux-Arts in Paris, where he was first admitted as a temporary student. He later entered the studios of Gaumont and Saupique and was elected *Grand Massier* by the sculpture pupils at the school. He was to stay there until 1948, submitting patiently and willingly to the traditional academic training: life classes in drawing, carving and modeling, working at the lathe. He received a scholarship, which allowed him to live during these crucial years of training. Then he had to earn his living by accepting temporary jobs. He devoted his free time to his "education"—experimenting with wire and plaster on a small scale, and attending galleries and exhibitions of modern art.

The César of 1948 was already subject to two compensatory influences. He admired the works of Michelangelo for the tension of their masses; the controlled elegance within gigantic proportions;

for the life with which he imbued the marble forms without, however, completely detaching them from the material, denaturing it, or falsifying its reality. A great sculptor never loses contact with his material—he intensifies its expressiveness without destroying its identity. César, whether working in scrap-iron, plastic, or crystal, was never to forget the lesson of Michelangelo.

Among sculptures by painters, the work of Picasso fascinated César most. In it he discovered the inherent dignity of discarded rubbish, the potential for heightened expressivity in the ordinary object and the metamorphosis in its appearance brought about by the unexpected bursting forth of the poetic image as a result of the elaboration and assemblage of elements. As a counterpart, of course, he learned from Picasso the relative lack of importance of so-called noble materials. César recognized his debt and expressed his admiration in a piece dated 1955 and titled *Hommage à Picasso*. Made from two gas burners, it is a work spontaneously suggestive of the spirit of the Spanish master's ingenious assemblage *Venus*, but one which carries the inimitable mark of César.

Between these two extreme poles, César sought his path; he was open to all encounters and hypersensitive to the Paris milieu of the period immediately following World War II. The great names in sculpture at the time were Henri Laurens, Henry Moore, Constantin Brancusi, Alberto Giacometti, Germaine Richier. César lived for a while in Montparnasse above the studio of Giacometti, whose famous filiform statuettes made a strong impression on him: "The first time that I became conscious of 'modern' sculpture was on seeing Giacometti's sculptures." And doubtless he was already aware of everything that separated him from the Swiss artist: in César, the organic image is dependent upon the imaginary; in Giacometti, form at its most evanescent signals the anguished and fleeting passage of life—the imaginary gives way to the organic. A work of 1947, a seated *Personnage* made entirely of iron wire, is highly indicative of the ferment in César. The proportions of the limbs and trunk, the position of the head, the form of the bust, and the small of the back prefigure the essential morphology, the classical language of the future metal sculptor. Already the material is completely dominated by the instinct and practical intelligence of the artist. There are no falsifying analogies—the work is born entirely from the iron wire, and the material dictates the form of the whole; through the functions of each part, the organic power of suggestion and expressivity of the sculpture gradually becomes evident. One must wait for the *Seated Nude "Pompeii"* of 1954 to find again, this time in welded scrap-iron, the same technical achievement, the inspired stamp of the artist, the same true felicity of form. When one thinks that this preliminary work of 1947 was executed in a student's room where the bed took up most of the space, with a shoemaker's last as an anvil, and with a hammer and a pair of pliers, the immense demiurgic power that could transcend such modest elements compels respect and admiration.

Meanwhile, César lived—or rather survived—with a growing desire to free himself from his last academic fetters and formal prejudices. "I ended up hating the materials I had been using for years, the classical materials—stone, clay, plaster. I had also made sculptures with paper and glue. But the things I was dreaming of could not be realized in any of these materials," he declared in 1959 to Yvon Taillandier (*XXᵉ Siècle*, May–June, 1959).

The things that César was dreaming of could not be realized for a very simple reason: marble and bronze were too expensive. There remained scrap-iron. César began to work in this medium almost by chance in 1952. Friends who owned a small factory at Trans in Provence suggested that he might utilize the metal waste that accumulated in their workshops. He took up the proposal like a challenge and began to assemble fragments of machine parts, turning out a number of amusing, doll-like Negroid figures and experimenting with various techniques of oxyacetylene and arc welding. He quickly realized that he had hit the nail on the head, and had found his sculptural idiom. After he returned to Paris, he continued on this path. He soon met other friends who lent him the corner of a workshop and a place to weld in a metal-furniture factory. From then on, César's sculpture developed according to its own terms—the possibilities afforded by his materials and tools.

The result was the life-size *Seated Nude "Pompeii"* of 1954. This nude—still rudimentary compared with the fullness of such works of 1956 as *Torso*—marks the artist's definite conquest of the metal. There is an immediate suggestion of a corpselike decomposition of form that critics of the time did not fail to emphasize. Moreover, this was the beginning of an unjust misunderstanding among many who regarded César as an imitator of Germaine Richier, then at the height of her fame. A typically Parisian misunderstanding, a trap of appearances into which a number of critics fell. Those like Alain Jouffroy—and he, not until fifteen years later—who have publicly

Continued on page 22

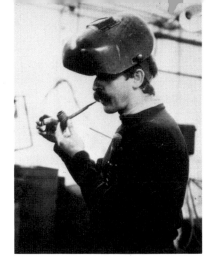

1.

2.

3.

1/2/3
César aux ateliers de Villetaneuse.
César in the metal-cabinet factory at Villetaneuse
1957

4
La première exposition de César
chez Lucien Durand, Paris.
César's first exhibition
at Galerie Lucien Durand, Paris
1954

4.

acknowledged their error are rare indeed.[2] In a book published in 1960, *Poétique de la sculpture* (Les Cahiers du Musée de Poche), Édouard Jaguer shows, in this respect, a precocious clairvoyance: "As with Giacometti and Müller, it was a different spirit that led the humanoid—but not human—creatures of Richier and César to a similar formal expressivity. Moreover, the relative similarity in the convulsive shaping of the forms stems from a common reaction to the degrading realities of life, generating an emotion that any artist cannot help but feel deep within himself when faced with the defilement, the mutilations and deformations inflicted on the human body by terror, fire, and burial—whether it be at Buchenwald or Pompeii." Let us be fair to César and not judge him by appearances. The 1954 *Seated Nude "Pompeii"* is a mass of rods, bolts, and metal plates that we perceive as such; however, it is from this mass of scrap-iron that the sculpture—that is to say, the form—emerges in a triumph of life over rubbish and inertia. Unlike Richier and Robert Müller (a student of Richier from 1939 to 1944), César, in this work, has absolutely no intention of attacking life from a phantasmagorical and disquieting Surrealist perspective or through an Expressionist vision of violence like that of the CoBrA group. On the contrary, he means to glorify life in an eruption of form organically linked to the material. Between 1954 and 1956, César's talent quickly ripened, and in two years he grew to be a master of metal sculpture, precisely because he was able to imbue his forms with an unexpected life through the free treatment of his material. Despite his admiration for Gargallo, he had resisted for some time the temptation to work with forged iron, a slow technique in no way suitable for the flexible, rapid, and subtle play of his imagination. It is here that César the welder is incomparably superior to González, the pioneer craftsman of the technique. César sets out to embody his poetic idea directly within the possibilities offered by the material, not to bend it to the pre-established morphology of a post-Cubist aesthetic. In the wake of Picasso the assembler of the 1930s, González, a true craftsman but a limited creator, could only flounder in semi-organic decoration. César's *Seated Nude "Pompeii"* of 1954 put González's series of *Cactus-Men* (1936) in its proper place, and established César as the master of metal sculpture—of a particular sort of metal sculpture, as defined by Douglas Cooper in 1960: "A sculpture that is directly hammered, welded, or twisted from any kind of metal, whether sheet, strip, bar, or wire." [3]

Sculpture in metal has had a number of simultaneous and parallel developments. The work of Alexander Calder and Jean Tinguely, involving the problem of mechanical animation; the kinetic sculpture of El Lissitsky and Nicolas Schöffer; the profusion of Expressionist sculptors working in iron, in a decorative style, in the Anglo-Saxon and Germanic countries, such as Lynn Chadwick, Eduardo Paolozzi, Hans Uhlmann, Clarke, Smith, Theodore Roszak; the satirical Neo-Dada "Dolls" of the Dane Robert Jacobsen; and the open structures of the American Richard Lippold come readily to mind.

It was during 1954–56 that César emerged, like a bolt of lightning, from anonymity in the Latin Quarter to fame in the Faubourg Saint-Honoré. In 1954, at the age of thirty-three, he had his first one-man show at Lucien Durand's, followed in 1955 and 1956 by two joint exhibitions at the Galerie Rive Droite—the first in company with Karel Appel and the second with Alberto Burri. His main theme was the bestiary, all prongs, scales, and armor, a bubbling scrap-iron mass of elementary life. Among these works are *The Bug*, *Scorpion*, *Rascasse* (a Mediterranean fish), the *Animals*, and the *Insectes*. "The miracle in the affair," as Alain Bosquet remarked at the time, "is that his woman is all woman, his insect entirely insect, and their components no longer nails."

At the same time as his *Insectes* and *Nudes*, César executed a series of *Plaques* in relief, evidence of a preoccupation with frontality. Jaguer has pointed to an Assyrian influence in these works. The persistence of wall sculptures is one of the constants of César's art. The principle of frontality is sometimes totally expressed, with metallic elements welded to a metal background, as in certain reliefs of 1955–56. Sometimes the plaque and its protuberances are inserted in an architectural framework, with the addition of rods to create prismatic volumes that open in space (as in *Portrait of Michel Tapié*, 1955). The same structural definition had been employed in a work of 1954–55, the *Chair*, in which a figure seated on a quadrilateral of rods leans against a web-like background.

Three outstanding works of 1955–56 mark the crucial point in César's development and prefigure the whole of his welded oeuvre: *Torso*, *La Grande Duchesse*, and *Skate*. Compared with the *Seated Nude "Pompeii"* of 1954, still somewhat like a robot with its outer layer stripped away, *Torso* of 1956 illustrates the artist's total mastery of technique and allows us to measure the distance he had traveled in those two years—two years of work in the factory, where César's imagination was stimulated, conditioned, and heightened by the very limitations imposed by his working conditions. He had nothing with which to create except what he found in the factory. The ability he developed to extract the best aspect of any material whatsoever is the secret of the inner vitality of César's sculptures, of their bursting humanity. He had no other choice but to overcome the difficulties inherent in his basic elements.

The headless *Torso* terminates in the stumps of the thighs. It has only one arm, and its entrails are exposed on one side, allowing a glimpse into an intestinal maze of rods and tubes. But the rugged contour of stomach and breasts foreshadows undeniably the triumphant and glorified humanity of the later masterpieces in this vein: *The Venus of Villetaneuse* (1962) and *The Victory of Villetaneuse* (1965). *La Grande Duchesse* and the *Skate* bring this phase to a close on a note of virtuosity: *the transition from the use of pieces of scrap-iron to a homogenous metal substance is henceforth accomplished.*

César could no longer be accused of the ugly practice of Art Brut. Nor could he be treated as though he were a three-dimensional plagiarist of Dubuffet. Certain of his humorous early attempts —a sculptural assemblage like the *Marionnettes* of 1955—may suggest the grotesque and erroneously childish figures that Dubuffet skillfully scratched on his high-impasto surfaces. With César it was a playful idea, a passing fancy, a flight of imaginative fantasy that he was to indulge many times. But what a difference between César's *Nudes* and Dubuffet's *Corps de dames*! Dubuffet adulterates the image that he "deculturalizes" by camouflaging the drawing and falsifying the painting—"*merde* in a silk stocking," as Napoleon said of Talleyrand. César begins with the reality of the scrap-iron, and, as a result of the organic exuberance of the forms he creates, his sculptures achieve a life-like realism.

Continued on page 85

5
Personnage
1947

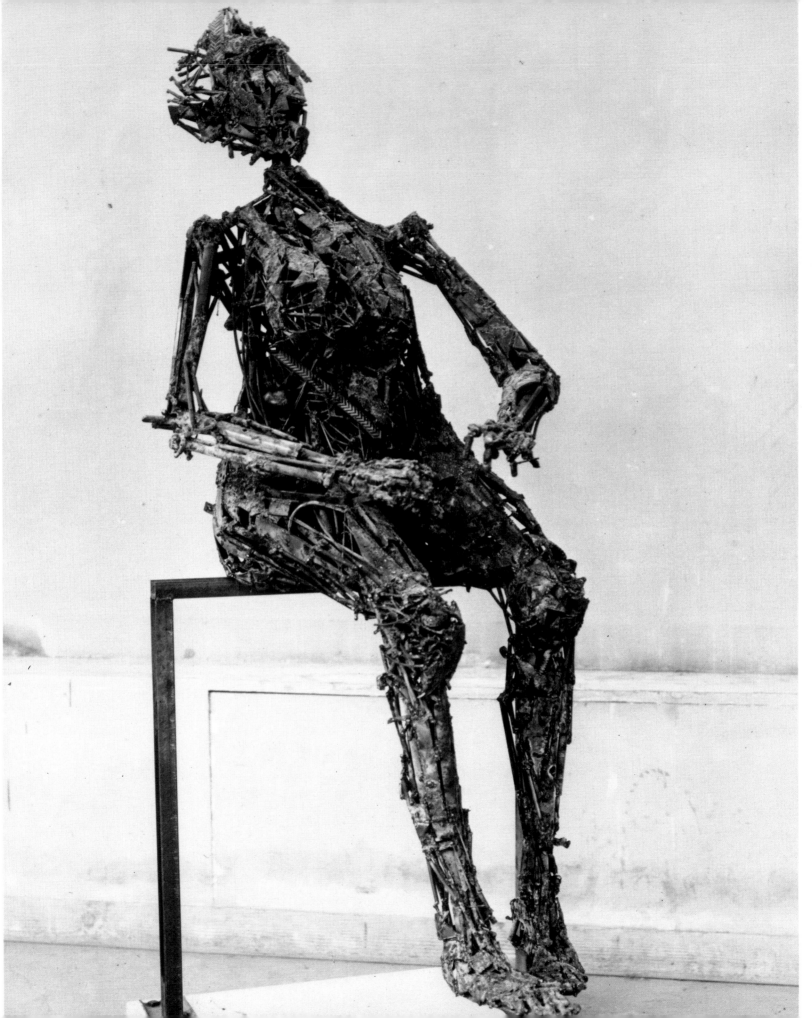

26

6
Nu assis
« Pompéi »
Seated Nude
« Pompeii »
1954

7 ▶
Échassier
Wading Bird
1959

28

8
La Cocotte
Bird
1964

9 ▶
Nu assis
Seated Nude
1956

31

◄ 10
Insecte
1955

11
Petite Boîte
Small Box
1959

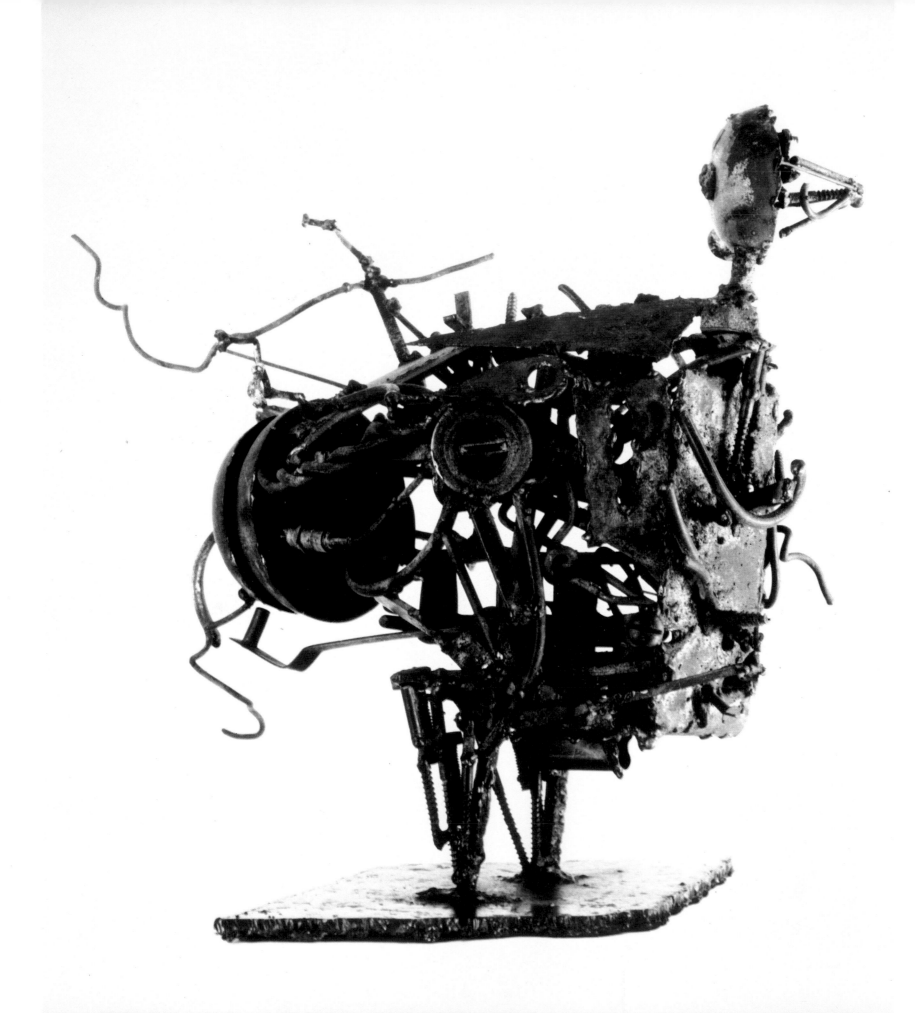

32

33

◄ 12
Poule
Hen
1954

13
Tubes écrasés
Crushed Tubes
1954

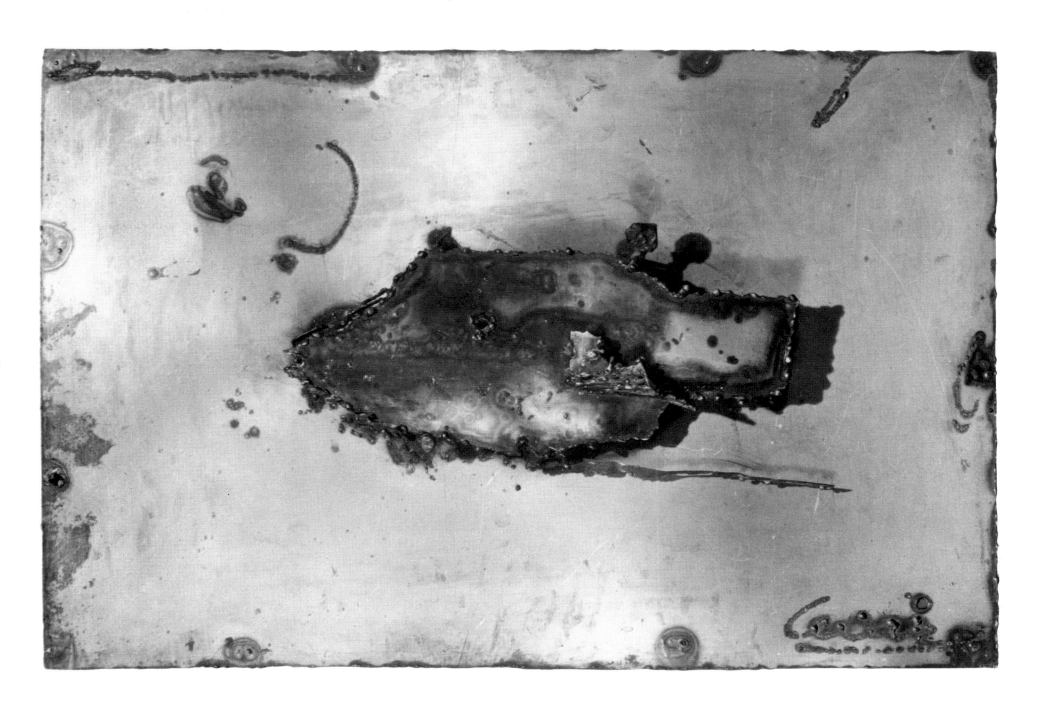

34

14
Relief au Poisson
Relief with Fish
1954

15 ▶
Hommage à Picasso
1955

16
La Punaise
The Bug
1955

17 ▶
Portrait de Patrick Waldberg
1961

◄ 18
Bas-relief
1961

19
Tiroir
Drawer
1962

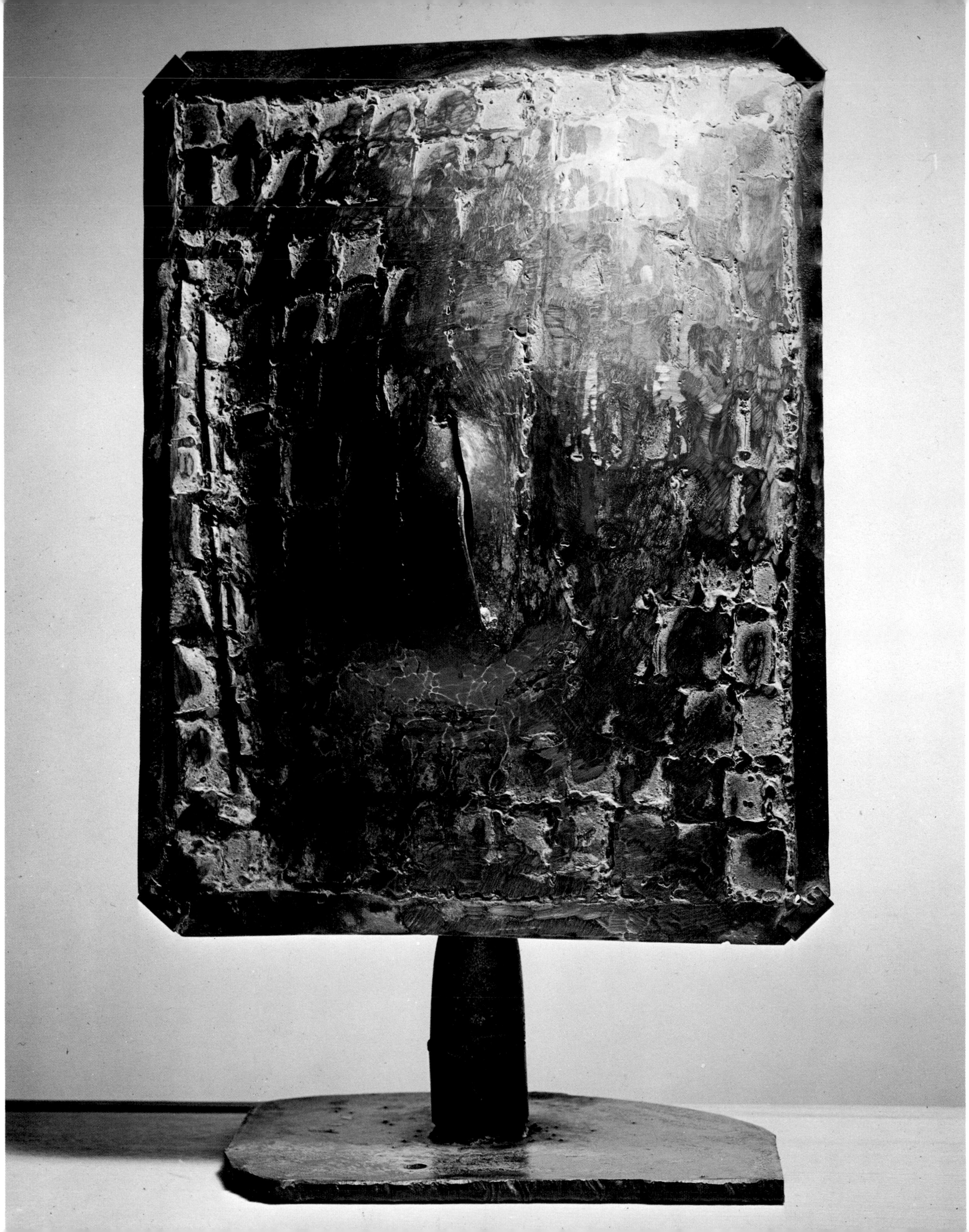

41

◄ 20
Mounine
1957

21
Plaque relief
1955

22
Insecte éléphant
1954

23 ▶
Plaque relief
1956

43

44

24
La Grande Duchesse
1955-56

25 ▶
Papiers arrachés
Torn Papers
1961

45

47

26
Valentin
1955

48

27
La Petite
Little One
1958

28 ▶
L'Homme de Draguignan
The Man of Draguignan
1957

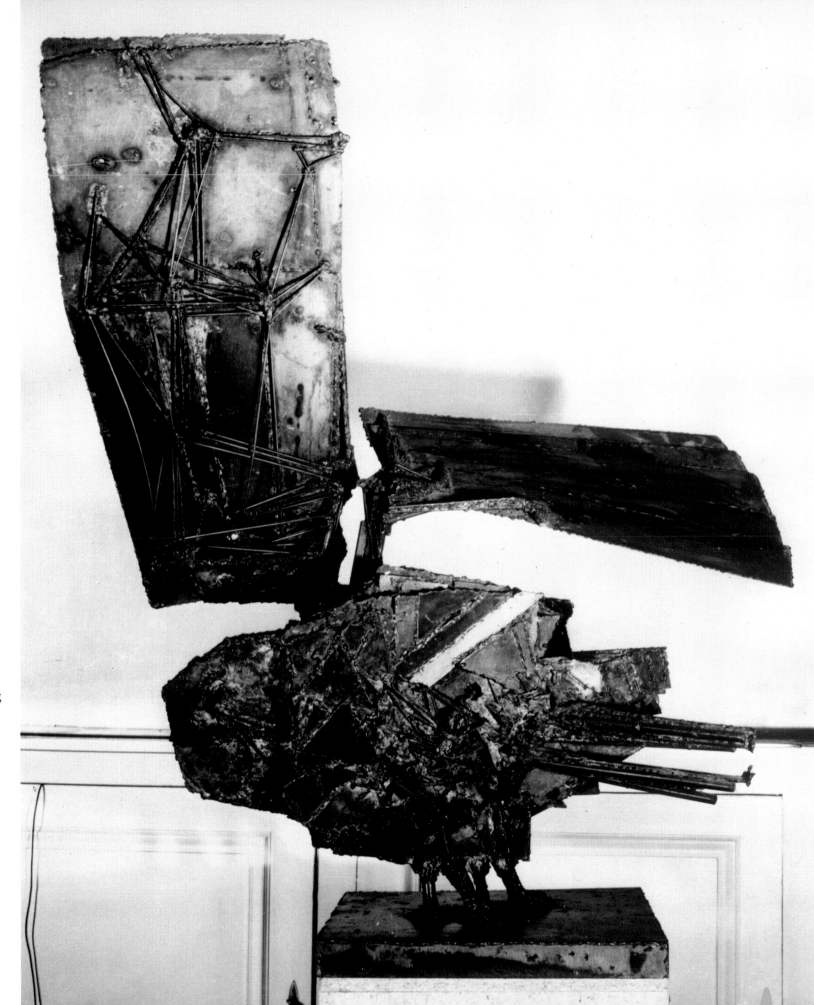

◀ 29
Valentin
1956

30
L'Aile
The Wing
1955

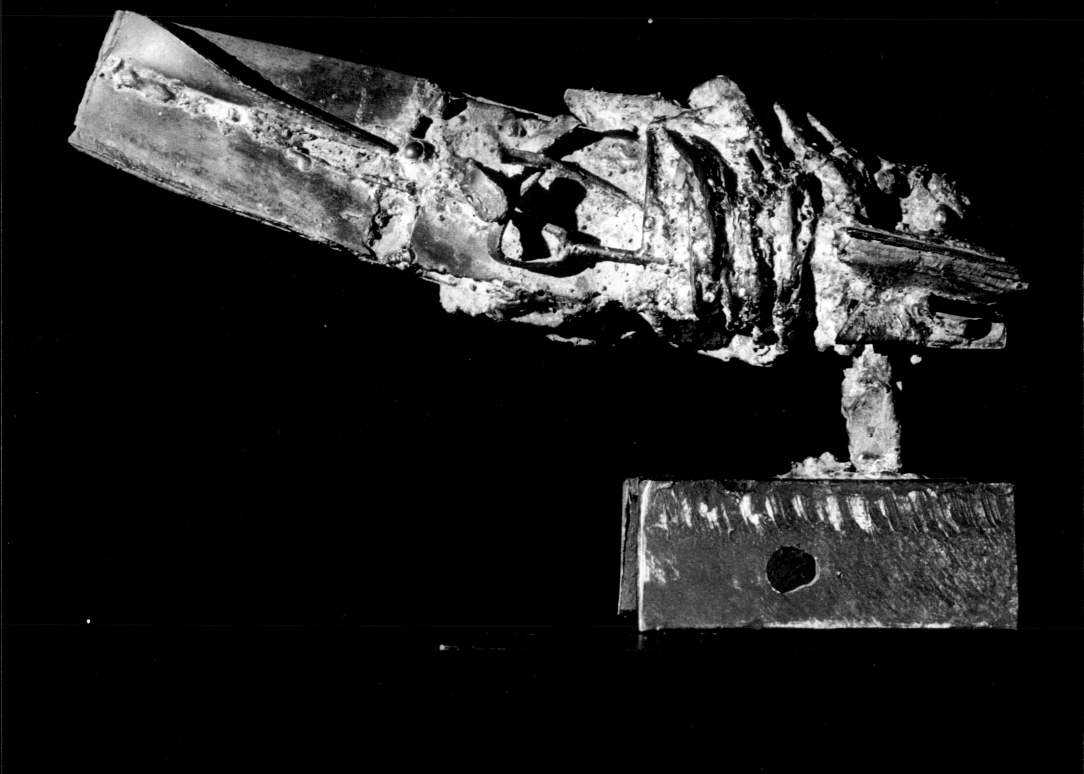

53

◄ 31
Insecte
1958

32
Insecte
1959

◀ 33
Valentin I
1956

34
L'Homme de Villetaneuse
The Man of Villetaneuse
1959

56

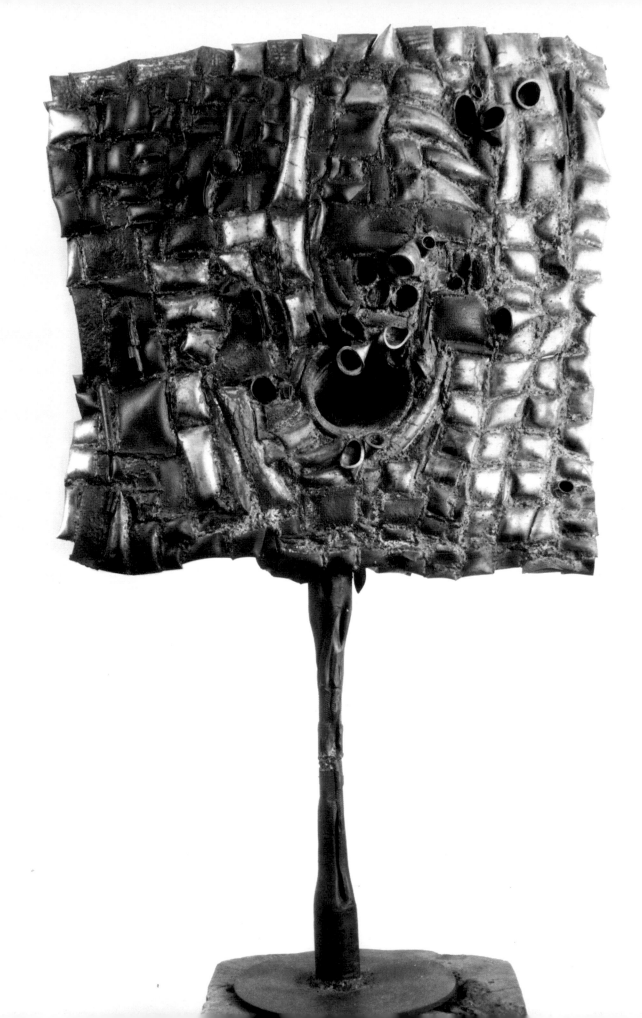

◀ 35
L'Aile
The Wing
1957

36
Sculpture plate
Flat Sculpture
1958

59

38
Sculpture plate
Flat Sculpture
1958
(Détail page 58)

39
Petite Plaque n° 1
Small Plaque No. 1
1960
(Détail page 60)

40
La Petite Fenêtre
The Little Window
1959
(Détail page 61)

41
Femme
Woman
1963
(Détail page 62)

42
L'Homme de Figanières
The Man of Figanières
1964
(Détail page 63)

60

61

48
Marseille
1960
◄(Détail)

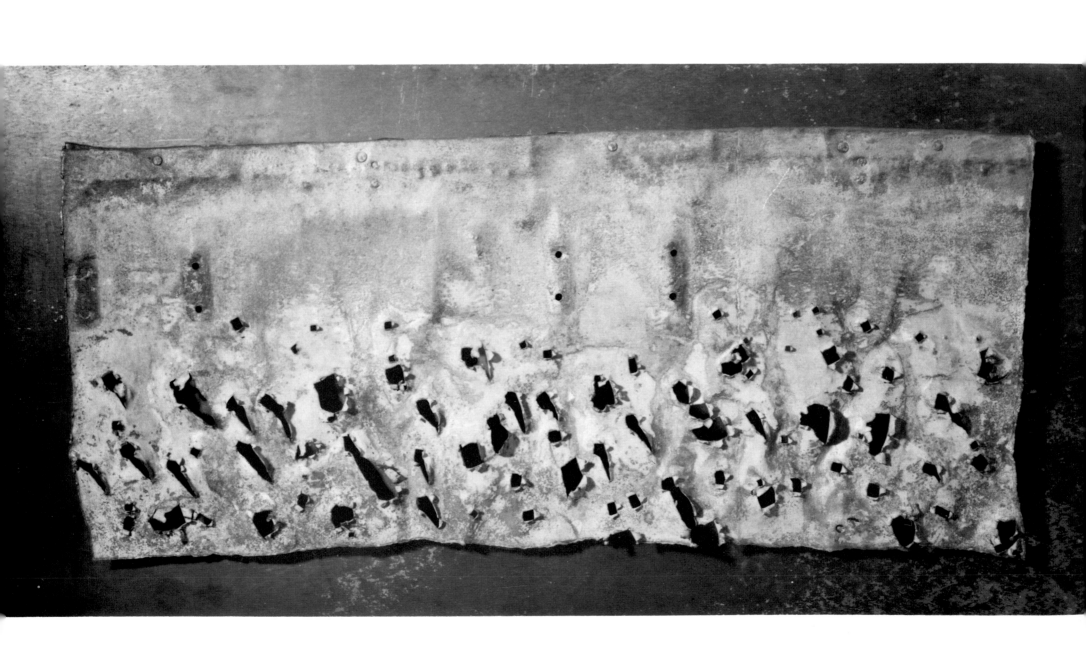

◄ 49
Râpe longue
Long File
1960

50
Râpe ronde
Round File
1960

68

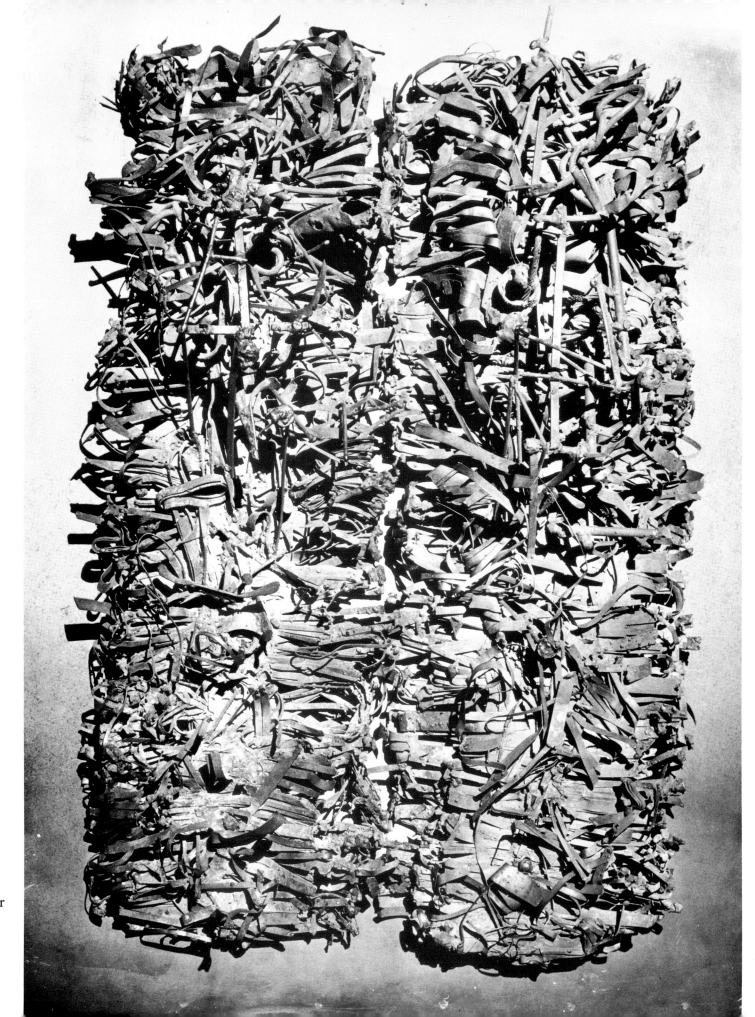

69

◄ 51
La Sœur de l'autre
The Other One's Sister
1962

52
Bouquet
1960-67

53
Hommage
1960

54 ▶
Triptyque nº 1
1962

73

◄ 55
Armandine
1958-63

56
César dans son atelier
à Villetaneuse
travaillant sur *Armandine*.
César in his studio
at Villetaneuse
working on *Armandine*
1963

57
Portrait
1963

58 ▶
Torse
Torso
1956

59/60
Nu de Saint-Denis I (deux vues)
Nude of Saint-Denis I (two views)
1956

76

61/62
Nu de Saint-Denis II (deux vues)
Nude of Saint-Denis II (two views)
1957

63
La Vénus de Villetaneuse
The Venus of Villetaneuse
1962

64 ▶
La Victoire de Villetaneuse
The Victory of Villetaneuse
1965

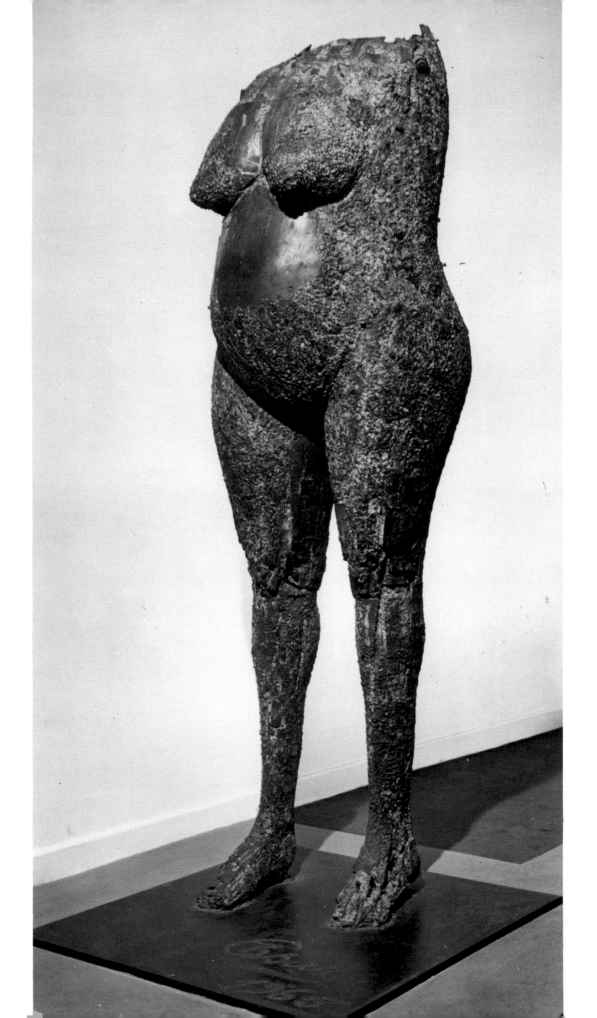

65
Ginette
1958-65

66 ►
Nu
Nude
1959

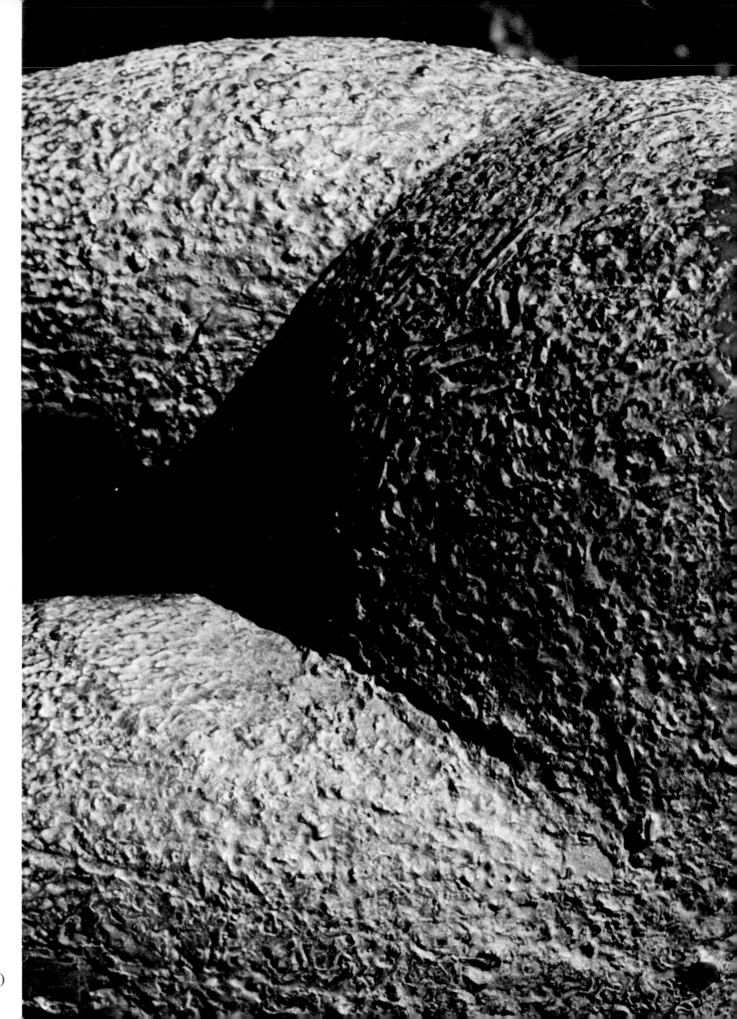

82

67
La Victoire de Villetaneuse (détail du n° 64)
The Victory of Villetaneuse (detail of No. 64)

68.

69.

70.

84

68
César à la ferraille.
César at the scrap-metal yard
1961

69
César dans son atelier,
rue Campagne-Première, Paris.
César in his studio,
rue Campagne-Première, Paris
1961

70
César dans l'usine de Villetaneuse,
travaillant à *La Vénus de Villetaneuse*.
César working on *The Venus of Villetaneuse*,
in the factory at Villetaneuse
1961

The years 1957–1960 brought César maturity of style and social recognition. He was the main attraction at the Galerie Claude Bernard, which, after its uncertain beginnings in the painting market —and at the urging of César and Erica Brausen—decided to concentrate chiefly on sculpture. The sculptor from Marseilles became quite a Parisian personality. Too much perhaps for his liking, since he could well do without tasteless society gossip and the vulgarity of the scandal sheets. But it was hardly his fault that he knew the stars of Parisian night life—Gréco, Régine, Castel, Bernardins—in their early years when, like himself, they were unknown. The snobs he had once met by necessity now became his friends. He dined with the Rothschilds and with Marie-Laure de Noailles. His reputation as a clowning man-about-town grew in direct proportion to his renown as an artist, and the Southerner in him re-emerged through all his pores. He defended himself as best he could: "I was born in the country where they grow figs and not apples."

César had come a long way; when one thinks of his Marseilles origins, his native quarter of the Belle de Mai, one sees what an immense distance it was. It required tenacity, will, energy, and genius to survive and to establish a reputation in the Paris of the postwar years and the early 1950s. This was surely worth certain wordly compromises, if in the final analysis they can be said to be compromises at all. César, the artist from Marseilles, with a name worthy of a Pagnol film, is an authentic character with his own roles and repertory. He plays his part as one recites a speech, in the euphoria of the moment, adapting himself instinctively to his surroundings. The whole performance is a rather likeable one, but the Parisian cultural ghetto, a troop of petit-bourgeois pseudointellectual scribblers and third-rate artists, was merciless when faced with the success of a talented proletarian. César reacted violently when such epithets as "proletarian parvenu" were flung in his face, for beneath his jovial exterior he conceals a deep anxiety that is the chief characteristic of his nature. A personal attack or a false innuendo upsets him deeply. This artistic genius, so secure in his art, is defenseless in life, and wants to be loved at all costs. In 1966, the city of Marseilles paid him the homage due him—a retrospective at the Musée Cantini comprising more than twenty years' work, including thirty-eight sculptures brought from the four corners of the world. To a local newspaper reporter who came to interview him, César confided: "The main thing about me is anxiety. I don't mean only the anxiety of an artist always calling into question the problems of his art—it's also a personal matter. I'm always obsessed that I may someday be poor again. Don't forget that I waited thirty-eight years to sell my first sculpture."

He triumphantly overcame this personal anguish thanks to the arc-welding electrode: it enabled him, as a sculptor, to give his imagination free rein over his material. His virtuosity operated in all directions—animals, reliefs, boxes, parts of motors. Throughout the extreme diversity of his production in the years 1957–60 one senses the persistence of a concern for the frontal image. *Fish* (1957), with its rugged head and the long lines of its body, anticipates a series of winged and oblong forms that project into space, the most characteristic of which is *The Man of Draguignan* (1957). A previous work, *The Wing* (1955), is a stylized depiction of a bird flapping its wings. *Bird* of 1957 repeats this theme: the body, which rests on a stand, is treated as a relief covered with a confused mass of viscera; the wing is a bent form in space. *Hommage à Nicolas de Staël* (1958) constitutes a remarkably successful adaption to sculpture of a pictorial style based on the juxtaposition of squares of color. This bas-relief, foreshadowed by a few earlier pieces in the *Variations* series, introduces the large *Plaques* that are the culmination of César's frontal approach, their metallic surfaces composed of thin welded plates set side by side like scales. By building up the surface in this way, César was able to produce numerous variations and rhythmic modulations of the material.

These *Plaques* subsequently assume major importance in César's work, and not only because of their technical perfection as bas-reliefs. They mark the beginning of a new stylistic option—the quantitative idiom. The superficial observer would be tempted to see these works as the most abstract of César's classical period. Abstract or figurative—this question does not arise for the sculptor himself. The subject of the *Plaques* is the metal itself, the accumulation of elements, their juxtaposition, their quantitative expression. One senses here the birth of a new, or, rather, a complementary concern —the intuition of a higher stage of the material, that goes beyond the quality of the craftsmanship and the mastery of the craft—to achieve a truly organic poetry in the metal, its immanent presence waiting to be revealed. This search for a self-expressiveness of the material through its total objectification is attested to by an experimental work done in 1957, the *Petit Déjeuner sur l'herbe*, in which a crushed tin can and a half-opened sardine can are welded to a sheet-iron plaque. It is a remarkably anticipatory piece, especially when one realizes that it is exactly contemporaneous with *Hommage à Brancusi* (second version), a ball of rounded metal that is both a moving and a humorous reminder of the formal approach of the Romanian master. It is a gesture particularly significant also of César's profound dualism, of the perpetual readiness of his instinct for experiment, in a period when both his vision and style reached full fruition.

The sculptor's international renown was growing. As early as 1956, his works were chosen by Raymond Cogniat to be exhibited at the Venice Biennale. In 1957 and 1958, recognition and honors accumulated: the Carrara Biennale Prize, participation in the Padua "Bronzetto" exhibition, a silver medal at the Brussels World's Fair, the Carnegie Prize. In 1959, his show at the Galerie Claude Bernard was a major triumph. All Paris society crowded into the rue des Beaux-Arts, causing a monstrous traffic jam. The sculptor's fame spread farther: to London, where The Hanover Gallery devoted two one-man shows to him, in 1957 and 1960, and where he found some of his most faithful collectors; to Kassel at the time of Documenta II; to New York on the occasion of the exhibition "New Images of Man" at The Museum of Modern Art.

His success was such that it would have seemed natural for César to go on exploiting an authentic and original style, a style quite his own, "curiously free from all external influence," as Douglas Cooper stressed in 1960. However, the works of 1959 and early 1960 display a tension and an internal pressure that indicate an evolving search. This search was for self-expressiveness of the material—he had to discover the perfect objectivity of the metallic idiom. If César succeeded superbly where González could only flounder, if it is to him that we historically owe the first complete and homogeneous metal sculptures displaying an organic harmony of form and substance, this is because of his extraordinary skill in seizing upon the suggestions evoked by the material and letting himself be guided by them without preconceived ideas. "All these forms that are in me are altered in accordance with their needs.... A work can always become something else." It is precisely this perpetual readiness of instinct that drives César forward, never allowing him to be satisfied with a technical conquest as an end in itself, and that makes him consider his work from a perpetually evolving angle of vision. César's vision is determined by a specific dimension of creative space and time, but his sense of time is not like that of others. There are in him different measures, different rhythms, different working speeds, which mingle, intersect, and are sometimes abruptly transcended by a stroke of intuition, a chance suggestion, a burst of revelation. At the heart of this permanently active mental "laboratory" different creative processes simultaneously co-exist. César's greatness consists in not denying this fact in the name of so-called historical logic and in remaining himself in every situation. Open to all the promptings of the creative imagination, he refuses to disown any of them, either in the present, the past, or the immediate future. His true inner logic resides in this permanent readiness, this commitment, without retractions or disavowals once the preliminaries of the search and the doubts inherent in his first groping attempts have been resolved. César at work is both perpetually restless—because he is curious about everything and open to all prospects—and sure of himself, prepared to assume the responsibility for each new gesture without ever denying the previous ones. He did not get where he is through conflict, or build his body of work by denying its previous stages—at any moment he is ready to acknowledge the paternity of the whole. The contemporaneity of certain works of a very different spirit can trouble only those who do not understand the richness of César's imagination and the many-sided structure of his sensibility. Anticipations and backward steps, prospective hypotheses and exercises in style, run throughout his work. And so he will always be: I repeat that César, like all great artists, must be taken or left just as he is. To accuse him of opportunism, to reproach him for deliberately fostering confusion —such attitudes make no sense in the face of César's reality. And for César reality is his work, which exists in time and space, and which, ultimately, no longer belongs to him since he has given it to us to see and has opened our eyes to a new aspect of our visual universe. His vital instinct is unaware of forbidden directions; his creative dynamism is not linked indissolubly to the continuous and linear progression of a single idea-force or central concept, to that intangible notion that politicians call a "universal order." Artists, fortunately, are not called on to justify developments in their work as businessmen must do for their professional expenses. But it is

Continued on page 90

71
César à « L'Exposition de l'Objet »,
Musée des Arts Décoratifs, Paris.
César placing a television set on a scrap-metal stand
that he made for that purpose,
at the « Exposition de l'Objet » show,
Musée des Arts Décoratifs, Paris
1962

72
Salle César, à l'exposition
« Trois Sculpteurs »,
Musée des Arts Décoratifs, Paris.
The César room, at the
« Three Sculptors » exhibition,
Musée des Arts Décoratifs, Paris
1965

a sad truth that people have not understood how César's attachment to the totality of his work may co-exist naturally with his spirit of research and his instinct for anticipation. It is by being constantly himself in the least important moment of his creation, by refusing all obstacles to his imagination, by giving free rein to his thought in all directions, and by denying any notion of duration or anachronism within his work that César is a free man, an artist in the full sense of the word—finally, that César is what he is.

César pays for this essential freedom of creation: despite his fame, an aura of mistrust and incomprehension surrounds him. It must be said that he has not contrived the turn of events and surprises of his career. But the spectacular or scandalous side of this or that artistic gesture is secondary to the strength derived from the affirmation of his artistic idiom, and the telling impact of a new opportunity for visual expression. César seeks *and* finds. What he seeks is certainly not the notoriety imposed on him by others. Rather, it is the objectification of his reality. "Reality," he says, "is what can no longer be changed. A presence. When I am conscious of this presence, I stop. I can't help it. It is a reality. The reality of today. Tomorrow there will be another one. It will be the same, and at the same time it will not be the same. But there is always an accord among these different realities. Each reality derives from the previous one, and the whole only makes a reality, a large reality. The Mother of realities. She contains them all. It is there for everyone. You have only to look. Yours is there. You end up by putting your hand on it."

At the time of their execution, the works of 1959 and early 1960 may have seemed, despite their tormented and sometimes singularly aggressive intensity, like the caprices of a virtuoso of metal. The series of *Motors* and *Boxes*, works like *La Maison du Fada*, *Magic Castle*, or *Place in the Sun*, today attest to a long inner debate, to a fixing of the sculptor's sensibility on a vision more directly adapted to modern society. The cumulative intention is obvious, despite the extreme control of the volumes and the perfect rhythmic sureness of the compositions as a whole. These works are basically clusters of rods and crushed tubes, assembled with an eye to form and rhythm. The whole constitutes a unified work, but the constituent elements remain individualized. In *Motor I*, our gaze follows the sensuous and tortuous course of the exhaust pipes entwined around a piece of fender. This individualization of the found object, particularly sections of pipe, is already found in certain *Plaques* of 1958 (*Bas-relief Variation*, for example). Underscoring the frontality of the sculpture, elements are added to the metallic surface in the manner of a collage, without losing anything of their objective singularity, their identity. But two works of 1960, *Long File* and *Round File*, are most indicative of the sculptor's future idiom; they are pieces of sheet-metal dotted with holes, in the same spirit as *Petit Déjeuner sur l'herbe* of 1957. This use of the object borders on the Ready-made. The article is placed before us in its full expressivity—for which it has been chosen. But this individualized object, this piece of rubbish, is not anonymous. It is not a matter of a bicycle wheel or a urinal—of a standard object promoted to the dignity of a work of art—but of a fragment of the real selected because of the expressive power inherent in its destruction and wear and tear. Nor is it a matter of an assemblage of objects as in a work by Picasso, of a change in the meaning of the image as a result of the surrealistic alteration of its basic elements. César the sculptor chose objects that were sensually expressive at a certain level of deterioration and decline. In his constant search for "reality," his vision drew inspiration more and more directly from a new consciousness of modern life. Little by little, he saw his familiar universe—the world of scrap-iron and the factory—with new eyes, free of the dullness of habit. At the same time, though he had always maintained his independence, César felt the need to draw closer to the work of Yves Klein, Tinguely, and Hains—artists with whom he shared the desire to be integrated into and to express the realities of the contemporary world, to glorify it in reaction against the triumphant conformism of the established masters of unrealistic abstraction.

César became an established master of metal sculpture, but his instinct again drove him forward. He identified with the realist preoccupations of this still misunderstood avant-garde, and was struck by the achievements, professions of faith, and exploits of its protagonists, and by the strength of their will to appropriate the real through this or that fragment of it. New Realism was born in Paris in 1960, and César was not to let this event escape him; he would find, under this label, the recognition that he deserved. The die was cast; he had only to discover the element of chance, the object that would serve as a pretext for his future work.

Continued on page 101

73
César dans sa Mercédès
à la Société Française des Ferrailles,
La Courneuve, où il dirige une compression de voiture.
César in his Mercedes
directing an automobile compression
at the Société Française des Ferrailles, La Courneuve
1960

74 ▶
Compression de voiture
Automobile Compression
1962

94

75
Compression
de voiture
Automobile
Compression
1961

76 ▶
Compression
de papier
Paper
Compression
1969

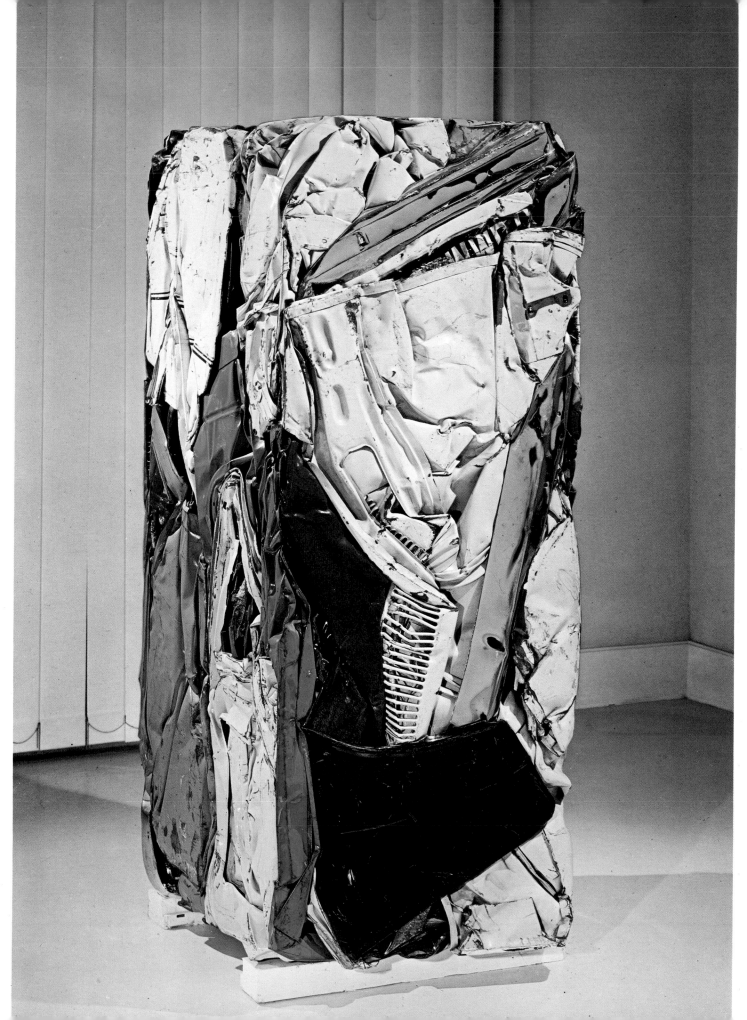

77
Compression
de voiture
Automobile
Compression
1964

78 ▶
Compression plate
de voiture
(deux vues)
Flat Automobile
Compression
(two views)
1959-70

Mobil
NET CONTENTS
LIQUID: 5 U.S. GALS.
GREASE: 35 POUNDS
GEAR LUBRICANT
38 POUNDS
17.24 KILOS

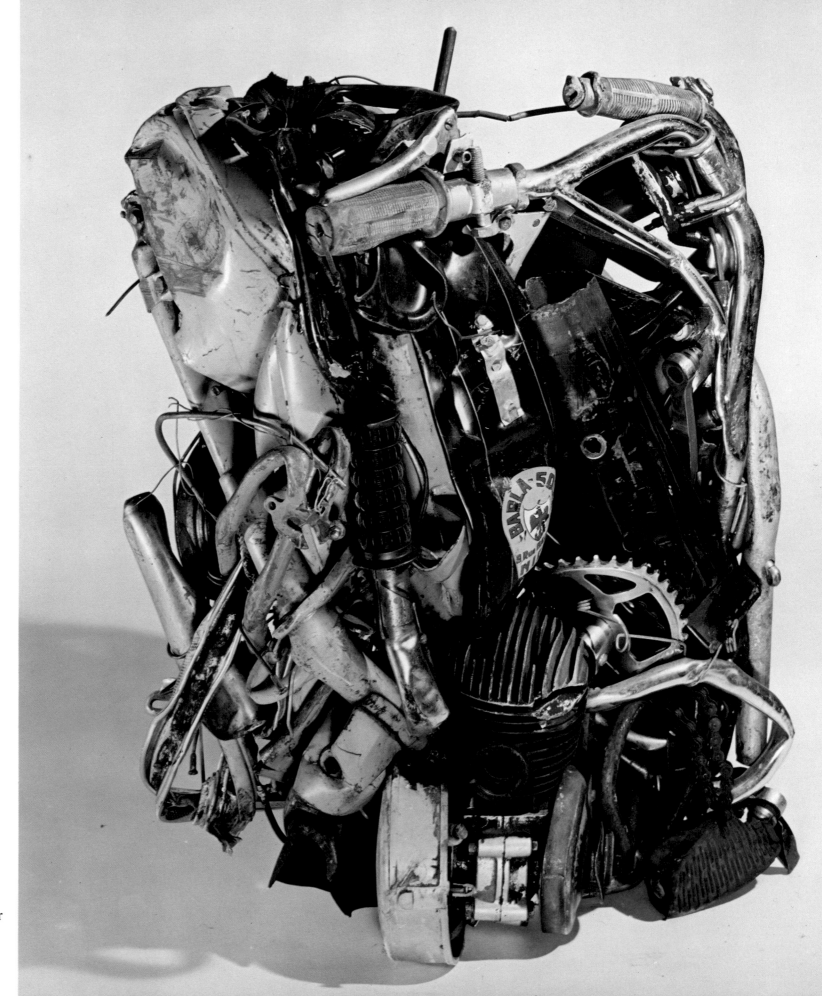

◄ 79
Compression
Mobil
Mobil
Compression
1960

80
Compression
de vélomoteur
Motorbike
Compression
1970

César did not have long to wait. In the spring of 1960, a scrap-metal factory near Paris installed an American press of the latest model. This event allowed him to realize his dream. The machine, whose vat was fed by a system of cranes with magnetized heads, compressed the scrap-iron into bales of different weights and sizes. There was a little of everything in the Gennevilliers factory, a true paradise of metal: bicycles, kitchen ranges and old refrigerators, saucepans and stovepipes, but especially cars. The cars swallowed up by the machine re-emerged in the form of polychrome prisms of compressed metal weighing close to a ton. This spectacular operation fascinated César. One day in April, 1960, he could no longer contain himself and came running to me to let me share his dazzling discovery. Art for César is the language of celebration; visual metamorphosis is a rite of collective participation, a little like a banquet. When César discovers a new aspect of reality, he is quick to show it to others so that they may join in his emotion and fascination.

I thus saw César as he surveyed the work of the cranes, measured the loads, and awaited the result of each operation. With him I admired the incredible diversity of these compressions, the almost magical character of the whole mechanical process by which they were shaped. One cannot help but be sensitive to the *presence* of this ton of metal, expressed to the maximum power of its volumetric concentration. This quintessential reduction involves a generalized transfer of the total expressivity from each of the initial components to the new object. The sculptor perceives the compressed metal almost as an event that lies within himself, that in some way is the manifestation of his own nature: the passage of an automobile from its normal condition to a state of maximum transformation.

César did not try to resist his impulses, especially since the problem of the automobile as object had been troubling him as far back as 1959. Even at that time he spoke of flat compression (the crushing of an entire automobile from top to bottom, like a pancake—an idea that he was to take up again in 1970 at the celebration in Milan of the tenth anniversary of New Realism). He frequented

◀ 81
Compression
de motocyclette
Motorcycle
Compression
1970

automobile graveyards and lingered over smashed-up vehicles. At Gennevilliers, he yielded totally to this organic enticement. It caused him emotional upheaval, but in the end his Mediterranean temperament overcame the conflict, and his sculptor's instinct assimilated the discovery. Aesthetic judgment was joined to emotional élan. Some of the bales of scrap-iron were more beautiful than others. The machine turned them out at a uniform cadence; they piled up in monumental pyramids of the mechanical age. César's instinct distinguished some of them from the rest of the heap, and he rescued these from the anonymity of the further industrial processes that awaited them. These were more beautiful than the others—César chose them because he felt them to be beautiful, and they became his own. He made them his sculptures.

From the moment that he recognized their expressive quality, it was natural that César should assume the paternity of his discovery. Compression thus entered the history of art.

On May 8, 1960, there was a scandal at the opening of the sixteenth Salon de Mai. César presented his new sculptures: compressed bodies of automobiles, chosen from among the most "beautiful"—three bales of vividly colored metal, magnificent, compact, monumental, forceful.

It was indeed a fine scandal. The old men of the committee of the Salon de Mai took themselves very seriously in 1960. Their Salon was the annual event of the Paris season, and they imagined themselves to be the arbiters of artistic quality. They could not forgive César for what they considered a deliberate outrage against metal sculpture, a crime of lese majesty against the art of the welder, perpetrated by a master of that genre. What an ill-timed gesture; what Dadaism of the worst taste (the reference to Dada expressed at the time the *ne plus ultra* of that detestable aberration, anti-art) in a salon that was honoring the great artists who had died that year: Germaine Richier, Auguste Herbin, Jean Atlan. A remarkable coincidence: at the moment when one of the richest chapters in contemporary Expressionist sculpture closed with the death of Richier, César began a new chapter with his mechanical quantitative idiom.

The reprobation of the critics was almost unanimous. The most open-minded kept silent for fear of entering a dead-end street; the most benevolent predicted the artist's prompt return to his classical vein. César's anxious dealers self-righteously reproached him for keeping bad company and accepting bad advice. It was in this climate of hostility and solitude that César made what was to become a historical gesture—the first of his *Compressions*. When one knows the man—his emotional contradictions, the perpetual anguish projected in an obsessive wish to be understood and loved—one can appreciate the true importance of his decision and everything this gesture cost him. The hostile solitude that surrounded him explains to a great degree the crisis—interspersed with pauses and backward glances—to which the sculptor was soon subjected, and from which he would not emerge until 1963, with the first of his human "Imprints" (such as *Thumb*). It was a period of psychological ambiguity and profound doubt, and although César's vitality always had the upper hand and his accomplishments were many, he worked under much mental confusion. Today, his *Compressions* appear as the hinge of an oeuvre that revolves around the appropriation of the real and the consequent quantitative idioms. The objects that caused the scandal at the Salon de Mai are now in the permanent collections of the modern art museums in New York and in Paris. But at the time César paid dearly for the position that he took and for his assertiveness. These assertive actions were, in the mind of their originator, the sanction—spectacular perhaps but authentic—for a new perception of reality: a change in the appearance of the metal.

In the results of this mechanical compression, César was in fact able to see something other than the end process of an industrial operation. By pointing out the communicative value and intrinsic meaning of the material thus treated, he awakened the most neutral areas of our perceptive inertia and opened our eyes to a vast sector of raw expressivity, so that we could no longer consider a heap of scrap-metal in terms of its usual industrial destination. The material took on a new meaning, and, hereafter, we would always be aware of its quality of latent expressivity. We are and will remain indebted to César for this enlargement of our visual universe.

César's new creative vision overturned the whole history of metal sculpture. He fully explored the challenges presented by his choice of material, and his resultant expressivity took the form of general solutions to these creative problems, as he passed from the fundamental level of language to that of a true sculptural style. It was up to others to deal with particulars. Although César did not realize it at the time, his vision had attained a higher dimension. Once the crisis that had been the consequence of this change had been surmounted, César was to demonstrate again, with his polyurethane *Expansions* of 1967, the richness of his gifts, the scope for synthesis of his artistic sensibility. The *Expansions* in plastic and the *Compressions* in metal demonstrate the same total understanding of the problems and limits of expressivity of those materials produced by modern technology.

Compared with the whole of metal sculpture in 1960, César's *Compressions* placed the problem of expression on quite another level. The innumerable metal sculptors of the School of Paris —the Férauds, the Guinos, the Viseux—suddenly found themselves outdistanced on their own ground. At the same time, César set himself apart from such American Neo-Dadaists as Richard Stankiewicz and, especially, John Chamberlain, who were also interested in scrap-iron and automobile bodies but whose work remained closer to an aesthetic compromise. The metal assemblages of Stankiewicz, infinitely more original than Jacobsen's paltry "Dolls," are halfway between Surrealist cerebration and the speculative baroque tendencies of Art Brut. Tinguely has gone further by giving his constructions the supplementary and synthetic dimensions of noise and movement. Likewise, in Chamberlain's twisted constructions, composed of scrap-iron and elements of crumpled automobile bodies, there is a dichotomy between the Expressionist color and tension and the post-Cubist rigorous control of volumes. César's *Compressions*, in their totality, go still further, or rather elsewhere—beyond. One finds in the art of the Neo-Dada sculptors and their painter colleagues Robert Rauschenberg and Jasper Johns the same aesthetic, and the same self-limiting prejudices. The work of these brilliant artists represents the transition between Action Painting and Pop Art; they must be credited with foreshadowing the expressive possibilities of our technical folklore, and with using it to enrich their own pictorial idioms. But they have never tried to question the Expressionist hierarchy of their fundamental aesthetic values, thus avoiding the ultimate realistic consequences of their modern way of life.

The situation was different in France in 1960. As in New York, appearances seemed to confirm the hegemony of abstraction. But unlike America, there is a profound rift between the two postwar generations. The discovery of technical folklore corresponds in Europe to a spirit of rediscovered youth, to the reconstruction of the industrial and urban landscape that was destroyed by the war, to a renewal of vitality in the face of the immense possibilities opened up by science. For young Americans, technology is much more a part of the visual universe; it is less shocking and does not provoke the extreme reactions that derive from sudden revelation. America as a nation is at home with the industrial phenomenon. Industry is its culture. In having recourse to technology, the New York Neo-Dadaists have sanctioned an existing fact: the maturity of a visual culture and its resulting manifestations. From this comes the possibility of a less brutal and more harmonious transition between pure abstraction and the reality of the everyday object.

In 1960, the Paris public discovered Kandinsky at the Musée National d'Art Moderne, Georges Mathieu at the Musée Municipal, Vasarely at the Musée des Arts Décoratifs. But at the very moment when abstraction seemed to triumph, the younger generation —Yves Klein, Tinguely, Hains, Arman, Martial Raysse, Spoerri, Christo, and, of course, César—radically questioned the non-figurative hierarchy of art. This generation no longer identified with the acknowledged masters who offered an escape into imaginary worlds. It turned its eyes elsewhere. Far from rejecting the contemporary world, these artists sought to become integrated with it. Their outlook was inspired by the institutions of modern society—by the factory and the city, advertising and the mass media, science and technology. This avant-garde had found its protagonists and the general philosophy that shaped its vision. After 1958, its extremist gestures proliferated in the form of manifestos, performances, declarations of intentions. In 1960, events quickened; the artists came together and in October of the same year founded the New Realists group. [4] It is within this period of artistic experimentation that César's *Compressions* fall, between Klein's "Le Vide" exhibition in April, 1958, and Arman's "Le Plein," which took place in October, 1960. Two years apart, but at the same gallery (Iris Clert) in Paris, Klein made a tangible presentation of "immaterial," cosmic energy—the bare walls of the empty gallery sensitized by his mere presence—while Arman filled the same space to the brim with all kinds of junk. Such events symbolize the two extreme and inverse poles of the desire for a direct appropriation of the real. That the *Poubelles* of Arman were strictly contemporary with César's *Compressions* has a concrete value beyond coincidence: from such scattered and diverse proceedings the common denominator of a new sensibility and a new visual language simultaneously emerges.

Klein's monochrome paintings, Tinguely's *Métamatics*, the torn posters of Hains and Jacques de la Villeglé, and Arman's first *Accumulations* were regarded by the art experts of the time as gratuitous provocations carried out by bizarre rowdies in search of personal publicity. César's gesture, combining Klein's and Tinguely's appropriation of reality, took on an importance irrespective of the sculptor's reputation. César had proved himself: at the age of thirty-nine he had a name, a career, a calling. He had risked everything. His radical choice made a strong impression on the public and raised the discussion to a higher level. In this sense, his *Compressions* at the Salon de Mai constitute an important event in the formative history of New Realism.

Joining the New Realists group was for César a completely logical step in his choice of appropriating reality. Like all of us, he was fascinated by the personality of Yves Klein, but in a different way from Arman and Raysse—their attachment to Klein was somewhat sentimental, since they were all three natives of Nice. César's fascination with Klein also differed from that of Tinguely, for whom "Le Vide" constituted the revelatory shock of a new vision of the world; Tinguely regarded Klein's exhibition as the catalyzer of a cosmic sensibility—in short, as a determining factor in expanding the imagination. César, like Hains, first became aware of Klein through the prism of his own sensibility. César felt that Klein, with his overflowing imagination, was also seeking reality—the basis of all communication between perceptive individuals, and the embodiment of immaterial and cosmic energy. What creator has not dreamed of achieving this supreme reality, the Mother of Realities as César would say? To be able to act directly on the individual and collective sensibilities of the men of one's time is a fine dream among dreams, and certainly not alien to those of César. Various projects for collaboration between Klein and César were suggested at the time: saturation of the *Compressions* with blue pigment; capturing César's image in the body of an automobile. Unfortunately, none of them saw the light of day because of the premature death of Klein in 1962.

But César was soon overwhelmed by personal problems, by the direct and indirect pressures of his collectors and dealers who were opposed to the "new wave," by the constant hostility of certain critics who stubbornly refused to take him seriously. Too instinctive to follow to the letter a theory whose essential choices he had acknowledged, César surely had need of the collective security of the New Realists group and in particular of mine, if only to escape from his personal agony. But the definitive solution could only come from within himself, from his own reality.

It would take him five years to become fully aware of the importance of his actions—that is to say, of the total supremacy of the quantitative idiom that is the basis of the act of appropriating the material. For five years, from 1960 to 1965, during the most diver sified and perhaps richest period of his oeuvre, he was to give free rein to the virtuosity of his creative imagination. This refusal to regulate his artistic idiom was to be interpreted in different ways. Some accused César of opportunism and of willfully creating confusion; others saluted the apparent return of the child prodigy to the fold of his classicism. The more indulgent justified his most disconcerting posturing as a refusal to let himself be enclosed by one way of thinking. In effect, by playing in several keys at the same time, all of which were his own, César retreated into the closed time and space of his own creation, and the exploration of his mental universe came full circle. It required an immense effort of balance to exploit his whole repertory, and one to which we owe some of César's purest masterpieces of welded-metal sculpture—belated, perhaps, though no less real. *The Victory of Villetaneuse*, a monumental headless nude almost eight feet high, of truly classical proportions and superbly sensual in outline, dates from 1965. This work represents the apotheosis of metal sculpture, the brilliant conclusion of César's series of *Nudes* and *Personnages* that were foreshadowed by the iron-wire *Personnage* of 1947, the *Seated Nude "Pompeii"* of 1954, and the *Torso* of 1956. After an interval of ten years, and while simultaneously engaged in many different undertakings, the sculptor from Marseilles gave this dazzling proof of his classicism in metal. In no sense an isolated work, it is the culmination of a group of pieces conceived in the same spirit and executed with the same perfection: *Hommage à Léon*, *Nadine*, *Ginette* (1965), *Armandine* (1963). *The Victory of Villetaneuse* stood out as one of the masterpieces of the exhibition "Trois Sculpteurs: César, Roël d'Haese, Tinguely," organized in June, 1965, at the Musée des Arts Décoratifs, in Paris. It may be that César needed this tour de force, this ultimate recognition, to prove to himself that he had exhausted one area of his creativity and to enable him to tear himself away from the Villetaneuse factory whose name figured in the titles of so many of his works, thus bringing his marvelous adventure in welded metal to a beautiful close. And in fact he was to abandon it for good in 1966, following the execution of *Postella* and *La Pacholette*, his last allusions to the animal scenes of 1955. At the same time that he renounced metal sculpture, César broke his last ties with Claude-Bernard Haim, who had been his Paris dealer for ten years. Up to the last, Haim had believed in César's classical vocation and would never acknowledge the sculptor's appropriative and quantitative advances. What the respective parts played by César and his dealer were in this interminable misunderstanding I do not know. But up until 1966, César laid himself open to many facile illusions and erroneous interpretations. This, of course, is the price he pays for always being himself.

In the story of César's development one fact remains. His *Compressions* mark the transition to a superior faculty of perception: the transition from classical structuring to the adaptation of form—form created in accord with a newly rediscovered beauty. Sam Hunter was not mistaken when in 1961 he stressed the importance of this transition in his preface to a César retrospective of works from 1953–61, at the Saidenberg Gallery in New York: "We are on the threshold of an art that begins to move us more broadly, like a spectacle of nature."

It is undeniable that César lived this truth intensely in the spring of 1960. I was a close witness, and my deep friendship with César, as well as my absolute faith in the soundness of his instinct, date from this time. The artist staked everything on the future.

In April, 1961, César visited America on the occasion of his exhibition at Saidenberg's. As many others had done before him, César discovered New York. Despite the language barrier and the difference in sensibilities, he had the feeling of living life to the fullest for the first time. His customary routine was altered, but he was fascinated by the architecture of Manhattan, the gigantic scrap-iron depots in the Bronx, and by the monumental chaos of the automobile graveyards. He was also aware of the chauvinistic and hostile atmosphere in the United States—it was the middle of the cold war between the School of Paris and the New York School, and the great quarrel between the art markets and the dealers was being waged. But America had already welcomed the New Realists: in March, 1960, Tinguely had carried out his "Homage to New York" in the garden of The Museum of Modern Art; Arman's first exhibition at Cordier & Warren took place in 1961; Klein exhibited at Leo Castelli's; and William Seitz was in the midst of organizing his famous exhibition, "The Art of Assemblage," which opened in October, 1961, and included an important representation of the New Realists. This was the prelude to a series of individual and group exhibitions of the work of members of the New Realists—such as Arman, Tinguely, Raysse, and Niki de Saint-Phalle—that were seen in New York in 1962 (at the Alexandre Iolas and Sidney Janis galleries, among others) and later at the Dwan Gallery in Los Angeles. Finally, from October to November, 1962, Sidney Janis

Continued on page 111

82.

83.

84.

85.

86.

82/86
César dirige
la compression
d'une voiture à Gennevilliers.
César supervising the compression
of an automobile
at Gennevilliers
1961

87
César devant la grande presse
de Gennevilliers où il a réalisé
ses compressions de voitures.
César in front of the large crushing machine
at Gennevilliers,
where he made his automobile compressions
1961

brought about a confrontation between Europe and the United States with a show that he entitled "The New Realists."

César did not actively seek success in New York as did Tinguely and Arman. They had close ties with Rauschenberg and Johns, who exhibited in Paris and were to play a considerable role in bringing together the artists of the new generation from both sides of the Atlantic. But César had few contacts with the Neo-Dadaists and even fewer with the avant-garde experimental circles from which all the Pop Art leaders—Warhol, Claes Oldenburg, Roy Lichtenstein—were to emerge by 1962. César returned to Paris with the feeling of having been close to an important series of events. He regretted not having made a gigantic *Compression* on the spot, but at the same time he felt more Latin and more European than ever. This led him to create a kind of myth of the dynamic, colossal, harsh, and unfathomable America—the quantitative counterpoint of the America of the rich collectors who came to see him in his Paris studio. One cannot help but wonder if better contacts with people in New York might have influenced César differently and given him the reassurance he needed—in a word, accelerating his quantitative awareness. The question obviously cannot be answered. The long period of ripening, the welter of contradictions from 1960 to 1965—could these have been alleviated? The important thing is that César set his own pace during this crucial period in his career and again found his own way.

César's *Compressions* can be divided into a number of successive series: the "historical" *Compressions* of 1960, the controlled *Compressions* of 1961, the cubic blocks of 1963. For a time he abandoned the *Compressions* altogether, but he resumed the technique again in 1968 with different materials: light aluminum pipes, pieces of Renault automobiles, painted steel plates, motorcycles, objects enclosed in polyester. Those *Compressions* executed in Nice during the summer of 1970 were exhibited at the Galleria Schwarz in Milan in November of the same year. Beginning in 1970, he made mini-*Compressions* of individual objects (toy automobiles, cooking utensils) placed on wooden panels. The flexibility of heat-treated Plexiglas inspired him to create transparent *Compressions*, fascinating for the pattern of the folds and creases in the plastic. In 1971, in his jewelry *Compressions*, he applied the technique to precious metals as he had to junk—undoubtedly initiating a revolution in the goldsmith's art. Just as, in 1960, the Vicomtesse de Noailles had given him her personal automobile (a Soviet Ziss, the only one in Paris) to compress, in 1971 the good friends of Carmen Tessier brought him the contents of their jewelry boxes so that he could make *Compression* pendants for them—one way for them to show off all their jewels at the same time.

In his works in compressed metal César again faced the fundamental problem of frontality that he had encountered from 1958 to 1960 with his *Boxes* and especially his *Plaques*. (He continued to execute these *Plaques* from 1960 to 1965.) *The Man of Figanières* (1964) is a classic example of a César welded bas-relief assemblage. The compressed loads produced by machine in 1960 no doubt suggested certain earlier welded *Plaques*. The reality of the machinery superseded the fabrication of the artist—to such an extent that Daniel Abadie, whom I suspect of an excessive indulgence on this subject, could declare that "one could not properly speak of a gap between the Compressions and the scrap-iron assemblages." [5] Let us say rather that—once the emotional power of the visual shock was assimilated—César fixed his imagination on the very structure of the object. He no longer thought of the *Compression* only as an object in itself but also as a series of surfaces endowed with their own expressivity. At that point, the *homo faber* took over from the *homo ludens*. César could not merely content himself with the beauty created by the machine. But how was he to intervene? To rediscover the sculptural dimension at the heart of an absolutely mechanical technique? By exercising a degree of foresight that allows for the preliminary selection of the object and the basic materials. By controlling the machine in the course of the compressing operation itself in such a way as to make use of the specific resistance of each object. By utilizing metals of varying specific gravities—brass, copper, aluminum—in order to take advantage of the differences in their behavior under pressure. By acting directly on the result of the compression through various processes of crushing, smashing, and cutting, so as to set off certain effects of inner *tension* or to create new surfaces.

Thus emerged the controlled *Compressions* of 1961, true exercises of style and virtuosity in the skillful handling of metal. *Come Here So I Can Squeeze You* is the title of one of the most characteristic of these works. César excels in drawing extremely expressive and formal effects from the materials he chooses. On the level of creative methodology, this approach illustrates how the dilemma in which some critics had tried to enclose the New Realists—as a result of their pure and simple appropriation of reality—could be overcome. The truth is that the desire to appropriate reality directly does not exclude the clear exercise of choice: the movements take shape and are linked together in logical artistic statements. César's controlled *Compressions*, like Arman's *Accumulations*, the torn posters of Hains and Rotella, or the "wrappings" of Christo, mark the transition from the invention of the object to its syntactical articulation, from the Ready-made to the well-organized artistic idiom. In the appropriative act, the aesthetic baptism of the object no longer remains an end in itself but serves to underscore the value of communication by guaranteeing a whole new repertory of expression. Thus, from an artistic ethic and from the behavior to which it gave rise—that is, the discovery of technical folklore—the extraordinary renewal of our contemporary visual idiom was brought about. The principal merit of the New Realists lies in their resumption of the problem of the appropriation of the object at the stage of pure ethics where Duchamp had left it, in order to elevate it to the level of the intellectual use of language.

The period 1960–62 is likewise rich in relief panels of automobile sheet-metal, in which Ready-made elements are welded in compact assemblages onto a metal background. Such works as *Portrait de Patrick Waldberg* (1961) recall, on a more violently expressionistic level, the first wall *Plaques* of 1955–56. In the same spirit, César carried out a number of monumental reliefs, one of which, intended to decorate the reception room of the quarters of the French postmaster general, suffered certain vicissitudes. After being unveiled with great pomp in 1961, it had to be removed some time later when the ministerial department in question changed directors.

These works, remarkable for the vivacity of their colors and the twists and folds of the metal, have a spectacular and decorative effect. It is here that César comes closest to the Expressionism of American metal sculpture—to Chamberlain, in particular. Very significantly, these relief panels were conceived by the artist in terms of deliberately decorative criteria. He likewise undertook the decoration of the entrance hall of a residential building on the Boulevard Suchet—a vast modular assemblage of screws and fragments of blades. "You can even paint with scrap-iron, don't you think?" he likes to say when anyone mentions automobile sheet-metal. And indeed, beyond the purely chromatic effects, the twisted movement of certain elements suggests a three-dimensional Abstract Expressionism.

In 1962, at the exhibition "Antagonismes II: L'Objet," organized by François Mathey at the Musée des Arts Décoratifs, César presented his television: on a base formed by one of his controlled

Compressions he had mounted a television set with a transparent covering that made the entire mechanism behind the screen visible. Through the expedient of technology, the sculptor from Marseilles rediscovered all the freshness of his quantitative vision, and the spontaneous poetry of industrial folklore. *The Venus of Villetaneuse,* a welded metal sculpture over forty inches high, also dates from 1962, as does *The Other One's Sister,* a classical assemblage in the form of a stele now in the Rijksmuseum Kröller-Müller in Otterlo, The Netherlands. César passed without interruption from one pole of his visual universe to the other. More rigorous in form and more compact in structure are the *Boxes* executed in 1961 and 1962—metal drawers filled with scraps of iron welded to the bottom plane. Displayed vertically in a line, the pieces of sheet-iron set one inside another create the powerful image of an organic microcosm of metal, a surface punctuated by twists, angles, and folds. In *Hommage,* a box-like drawer mounted on a base, the effect is perhaps even more striking—a single oblong metal form, split in two, is welded at the center.

Despite the many works done in a different spirit at the same time, one can say that the first part of the period 1960 to 1965—more precisely, 1960 to 1962—was dominated by the force of impact of the *Compressions.* César deliberately applied himself to the problem of frontal perspective, as is apparent in the reliefs of 1955 and the *Plaques* of 1958. *Bouquet* (1960–67), an assemblage of metal strips on a panel, shows the continuity between the classical *Plaques* (such as *Orpheus, The Little Window, Marseille, Coatrack*) and the works utilizing automobile scrap-metal, in the light of the selective creative process of the controlled *Compressions.* The drawings of 1961, exhibited at the Galleria Apollinaire in Milan in 1962 are quite characteristic of this frontal perspective. They repeat in graphic strokes the accumulative structure of the *Plaques.* Many drawings of this period are actually *arrachages:* strips of thin paper, previously inked, were pasted on the sheet at the bottom and immediately torn away. The traces left behind reproduced the repetitive texture of the *Plaques.*

The years 1963–65, on the other hand, mark a clearer return to classicism; though one can still note the co-existence of highly contrasted works, the dominant note is anthropomorphic sculpture. With *The Victory of Villetaneuse,* the masterly conclusion of a dazzling series of *Torsos* and *Nudes,* César has given us one of the purest masterpieces of metal sculpture.

A work of 1963–64, *Foot,* claims our attention because in a certain sense it prefigures the human "Imprints" of 1965—a foot in welded metal surmounted by a long rod rests on a flat base. It is a strange piece, somewhat reminiscent of the sculpture of Richier or Giacometti that also stresses the objectification of a part of the body totally detached from its context. This work is executed in an absolutely classical technique that is alien to César's usual quantitative idiom. All that was required to bring about the encounter between this stylistic idiom and that governing the creation of the anthropomorphic object (which would follow) was an opportune occasion, a determining pretext.

Continued on page 146

◄ 88
Compression
1969

89
Compression
de voiture
Automobile
Compression
1961

119

◄ 90
Compression
1959

91
Compression
1959

92
Compression
dirigée
« Viens ici que
je t'esquiche »
Controlled
Compression
« Come Here
So I Can
Squeeze You »
1961

93 ▶
Compression
dirigée
« On est deux »
Controlled
Compression
« We Are Two »
1961

94
Compression
1961

95 ▶
Compression
1961

124

96
Compression
1969

97 ▶
Compression
1964

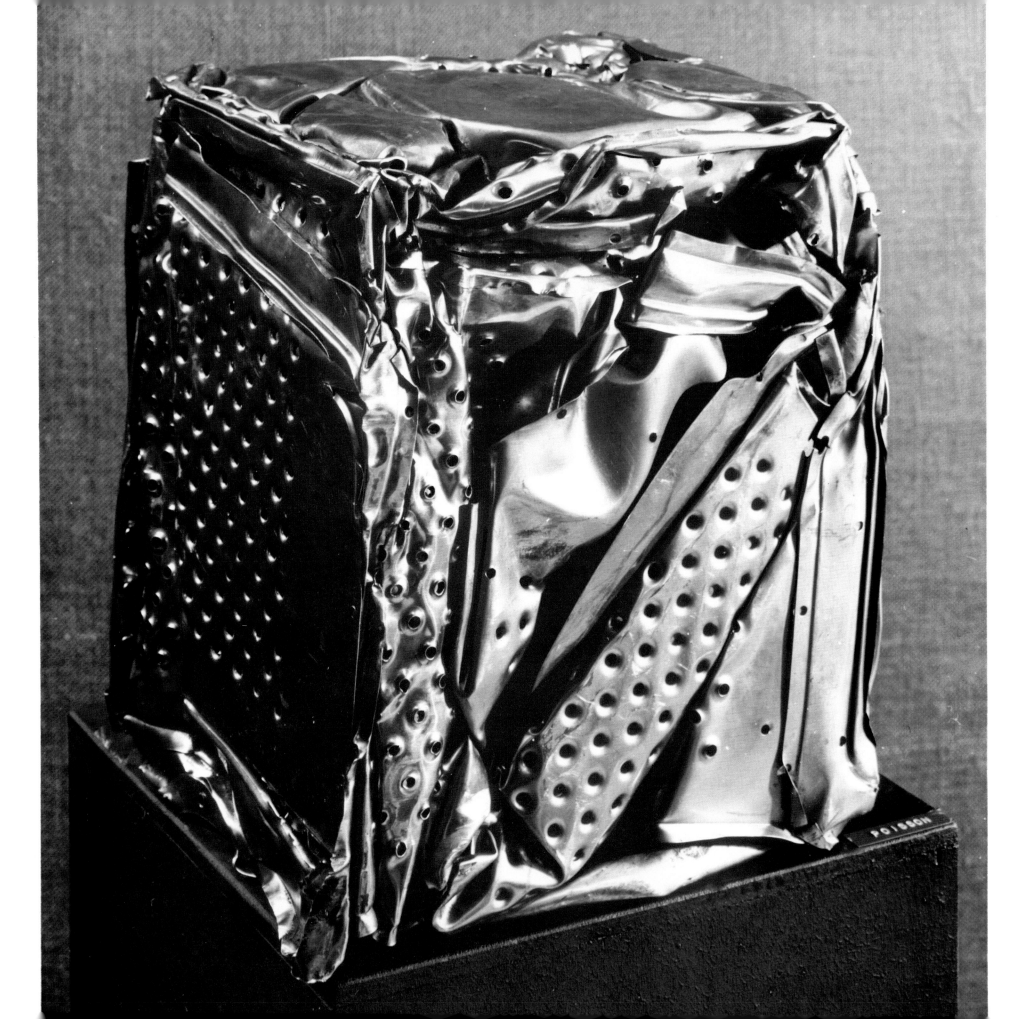

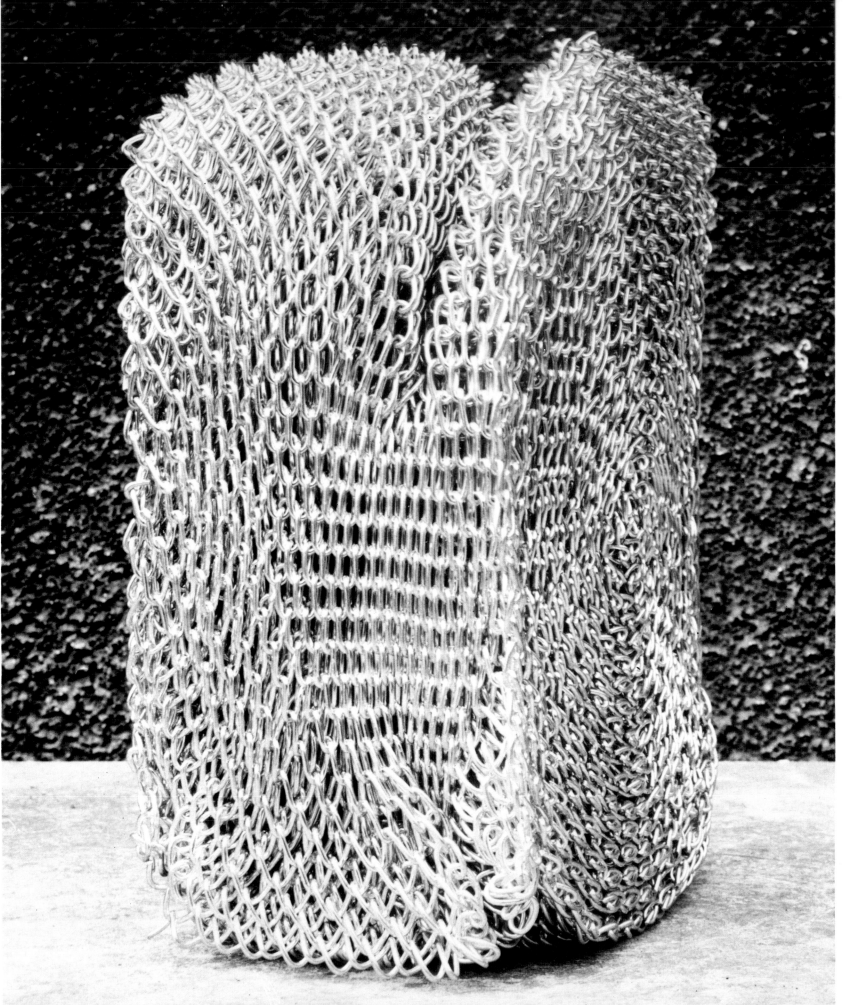

126

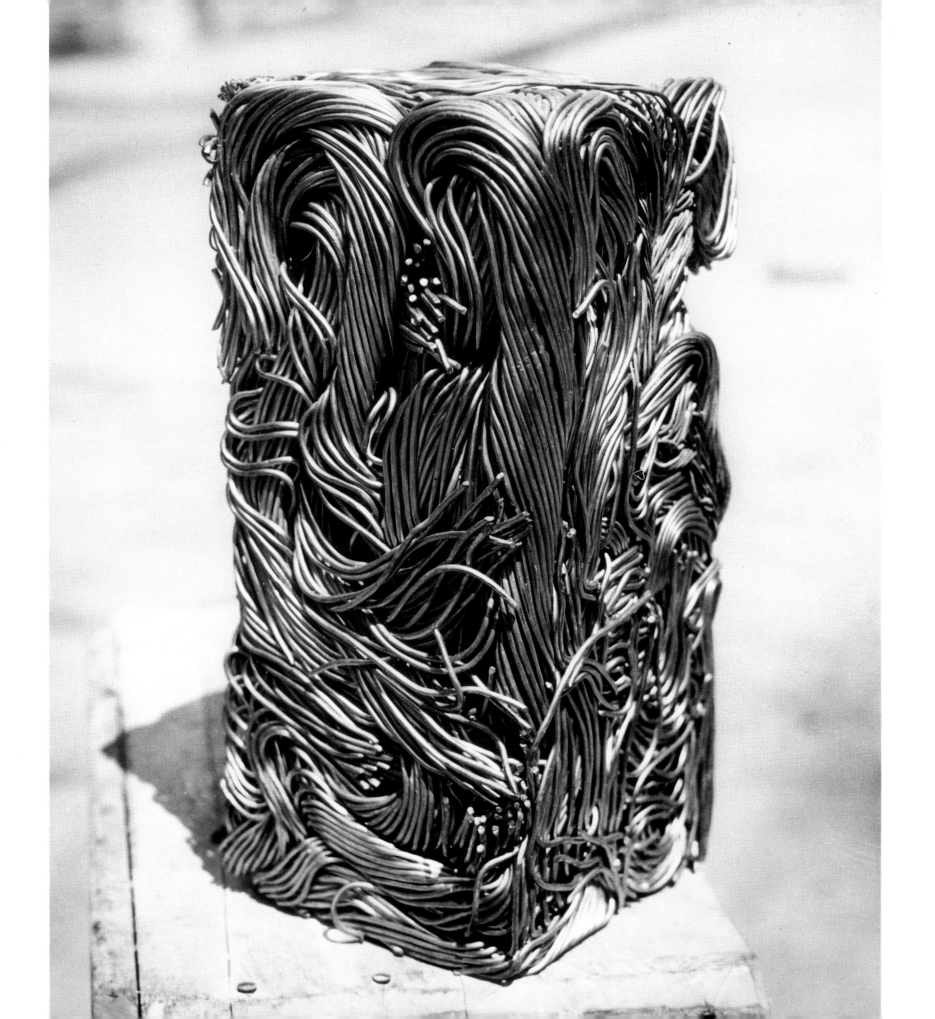

127

128

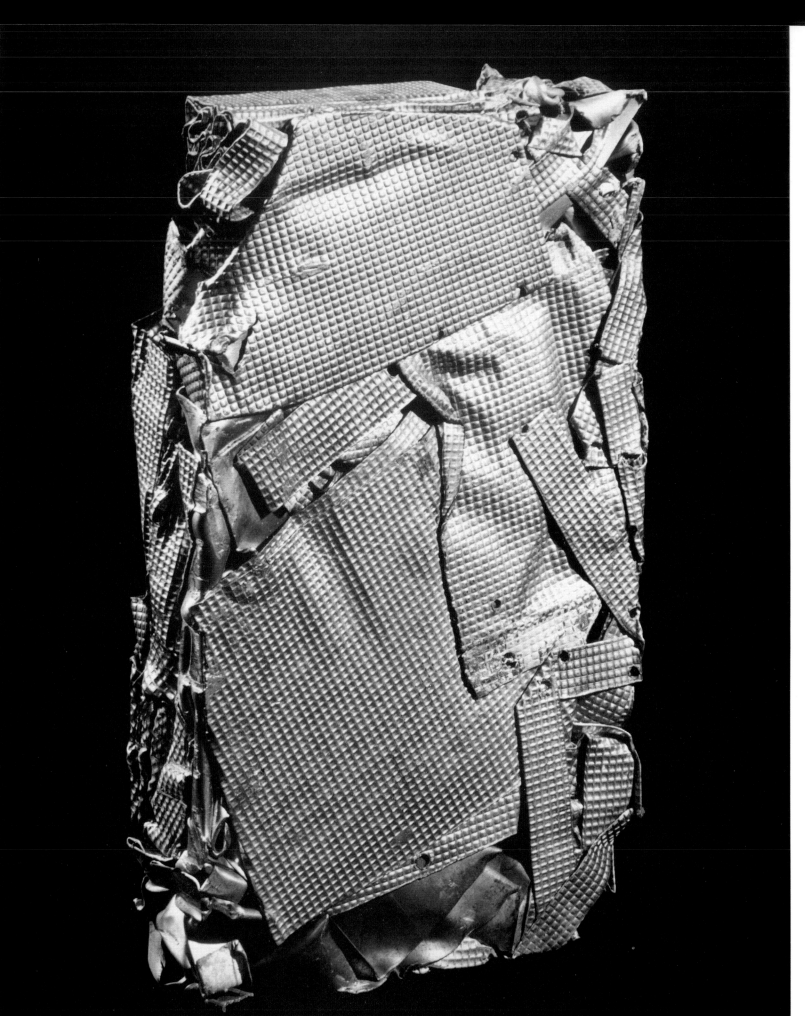

100
Compression
extra-plate
Extra-flat
Compression
1970

101 ▶
Compression
1969

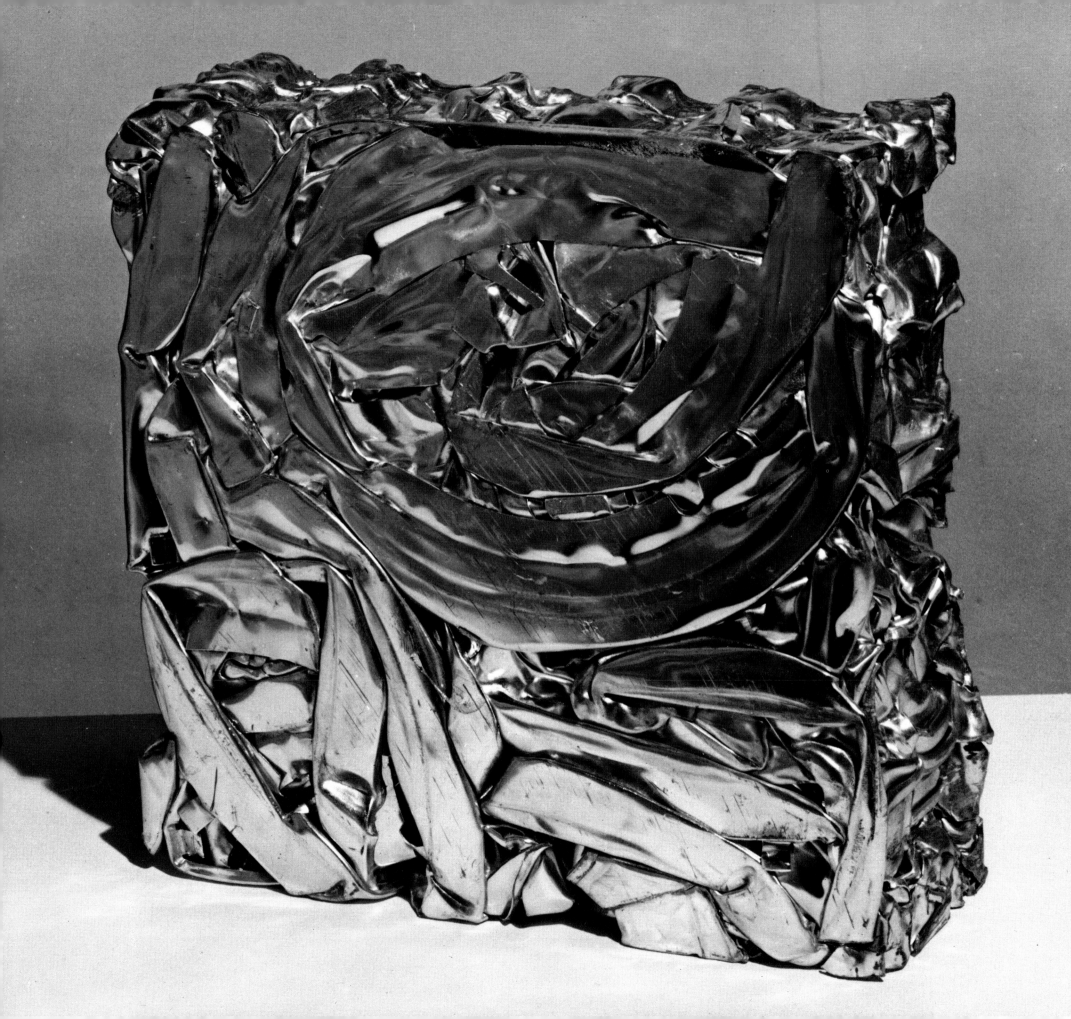

102
Compression
1970

103 ►
Compression
1970

104
Compression
1970

105
Compression
1970

106
Compression
1970

107
Compression
1970

108
Compression
de vélomoteur
Motorbike
Compression
1970

109 ▶
Les phases de
la compression
d'un vélomoteur.
Stages in the
compression
of a motorbike
1970

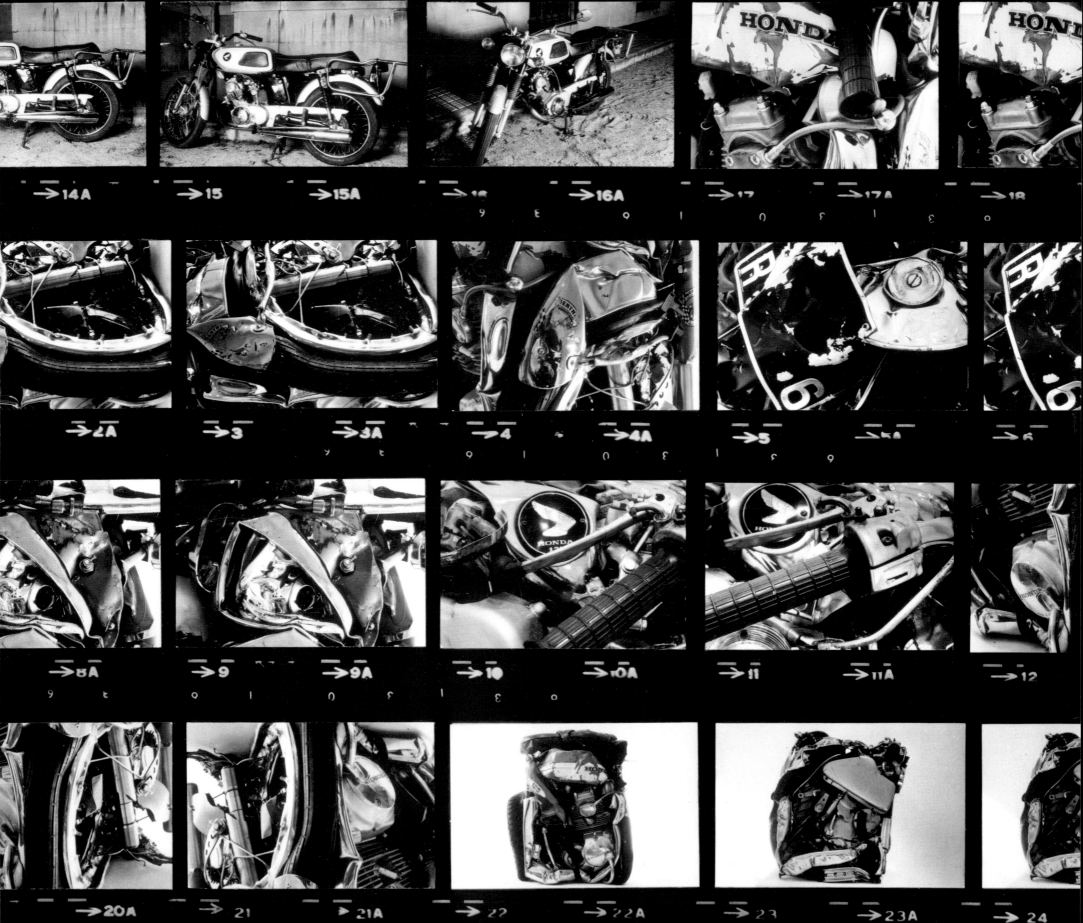

110
Compression
de vélomoteur
Motorbike
Compression
1970

111 ▶
Compression
de motocyclette
Motorcycle
Compression
1971

138

112
Compression
de vélomoteur
Motorbike
Compression
1970

113 ▶
La Pacholette
1966

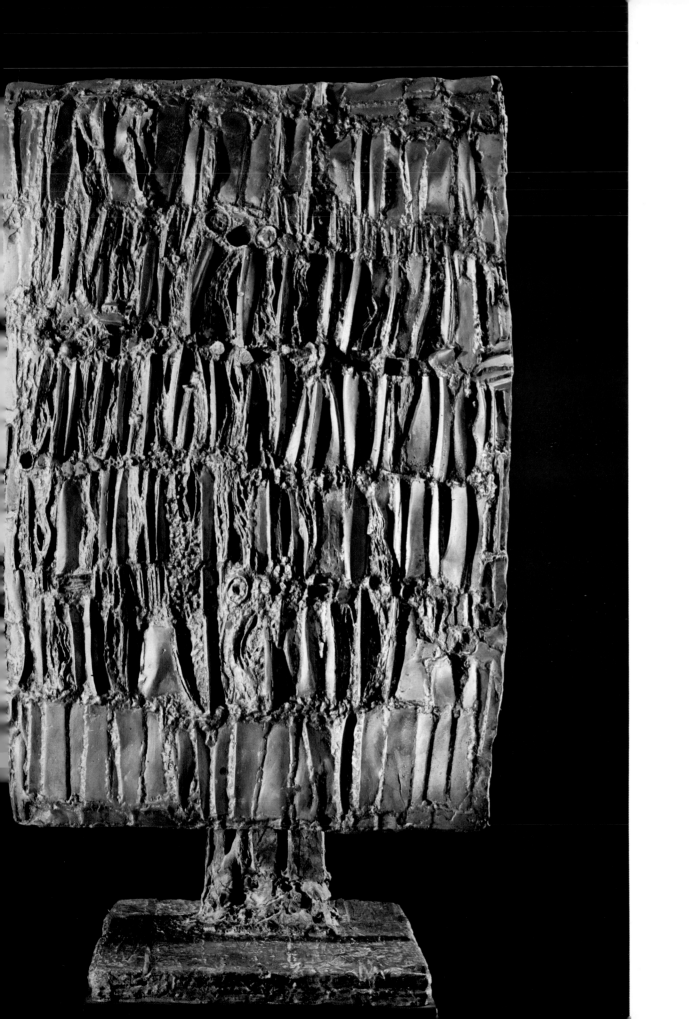

114
Pied de vestiaire
Coatrack
1960

115 ▶
Le Corbeau
The Crow
1955

116
Sein
Breast
1967

117
César (à gauche) avec la première fonte
en plastique du *Pouce* (1965),
Biennale de São Paulo.
César (left) with the first
plastic cast of *Thumb* (1965),
São Paulo Bienal
1967

143

118/119
Réalisation du *Sein de femme*, Paris.
The completion of *Breast*, Paris
1967

120
Pouce
Thumb
1963

121 ▶
Sein
Breast
1967

At the end of 1965, Galerie Claude Bernard organized an international exhibition of sculpture on the theme of the hand, bringing together works by the greatest contemporary masters. It was expected that César, after his exhibition (together with Tinguely and Roël d'Haese) at the Musée des Arts Décoratifs, would once again affirm his attachment to the classicism of metal sculpture. The fact that the forecasts were wrong caused a sensation. Kenneth Armitage, Lynn Chadwick, Jacques Delahaye and Étienne-Martin were eclipsed; Rodin, Picasso, and Giacometti, the Cascellas and Pomodoros, no longer mattered. And all because of César, who created the event of the year by presenting the cast of his own thumb, enlarged to almost sixteen inches in height, in pink transparent plastic. And this represented only one stage—the final version reached a height of over six feet.

To achieve this result, César first cast his thumb in plaster, and then employed a pantograph, a device for transferring the contours of a small model to a larger scale. The procedure is a traditional one when making large sculptures based on small models, and is ordinarily used for monumental statuary. César reversed the roles: he used the pantograph as a true creative implement, not simply as an instrument for reproduction on a larger scale. In fact, it was the pantograph that quantitatively created the work; César knew that it was the apparatus that had led him to the qualitative threshold beyond which quantity begins to "speak." "If there is nothing more antisculpture than a human imprint," he says, "I feel that by developing my imprint on that scale, I make it become sculpture."

While remaining within the scope of an anthropomorphic vision, César again took up his mechanical quantitative idiom and, with as much class as elegance, began the second chapter of his oeuvre. At the same time, he took the occasion to restate to Georges Boudaille—who made himself a spokesman for the public's general surprise—his right to the free play of the creative imagination: "The thumb is a thing that interests me... they can reproach me for not having made it with my hands. So what do they make of dreams, of the imagination?... I don't want to specialize. I do as I like; I consider that this idea, which I have just worked out, of making a sculpture from my imprint, is as good as any other. I have taken the responsibility for this sculpture." [6]

César knew that people were going to complain of gratuitous provocation, and he hastened to counterattack. The intensity of his reaction is not to be explained as a mere concern for tactics. By assuming the responsibility for his new achievement, he meant to stress publicly that he had settled certain accounts with himself and that he was ready to set out again on the adventure of exploring the real. The *homo faber* momentarily effaced himself in the presence of the *homo ludens*.

Various casts of *Thumb* were made—some in metal (bronze, steel); others, more experimental, in plastic of different qualities: translucent and fluorescent, deep bright pink in color, soft with a hard nail, and so forth. César tried to take the greatest possible advantage of the plastics that technology and modern industry made readily available, to obtain for his human "Imprints" an organic and sensual material that would lend itself to curved forms. He demanded of this medium the same perfection of craftsmanship that he had achieved in metal. His experiments in plastics were not simply prompted by the needs of aesthetic refinement or by the attraction of a new and steadily expanding branch of technology. They corresponded to purely quantitative concerns. From 1965 to 1966, César's imagination soared. He dreamed of monumental "Imprints," of a "head of César," of a gigantic effigy-portrait of the American woman, for which the model was to be Jane Fonda—all these obviously to be on a grand scale. With such dimensions, the problem of casting arose. Metal casting is prohibitively costly. Only plastic would allow him to realize such dreams, but he still had to find a patron or sponsor. However, part of the dream was to become reality. In 1967, he executed another gigantic anatomical specimen, the *Breast*—the representation of a female breast over sixteen feet in diameter and more than eight feet in height. It adorns the pool of the new Rochas perfume factory in Poissy. On this scale, the breast has the appearance of a lunar mountain crowned by the rocky spur of the nipple—each pore of the skin is a small crater. Nevertheless, it remains a breast, perhaps even more so in its monumental expansion. It is, if you like, the giant symbol of the Mother Goddess. But it is above all an inspired Fujiyama,

147

Continued on page 157

148

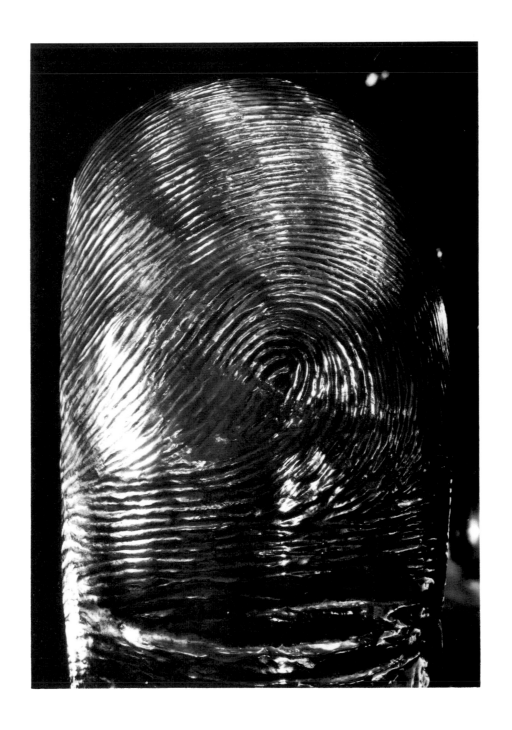

122
Pouce (détail du n° 120)
Thumb (detail of No. 120)
1963

123
Expansions réalisées en public
à la Tate Gallery, Londres.
César creating Expansions in public
at The Tate Gallery, London
1968

124
Expansion nº 12
1970

125 ▶
Expansion nº 16
1970

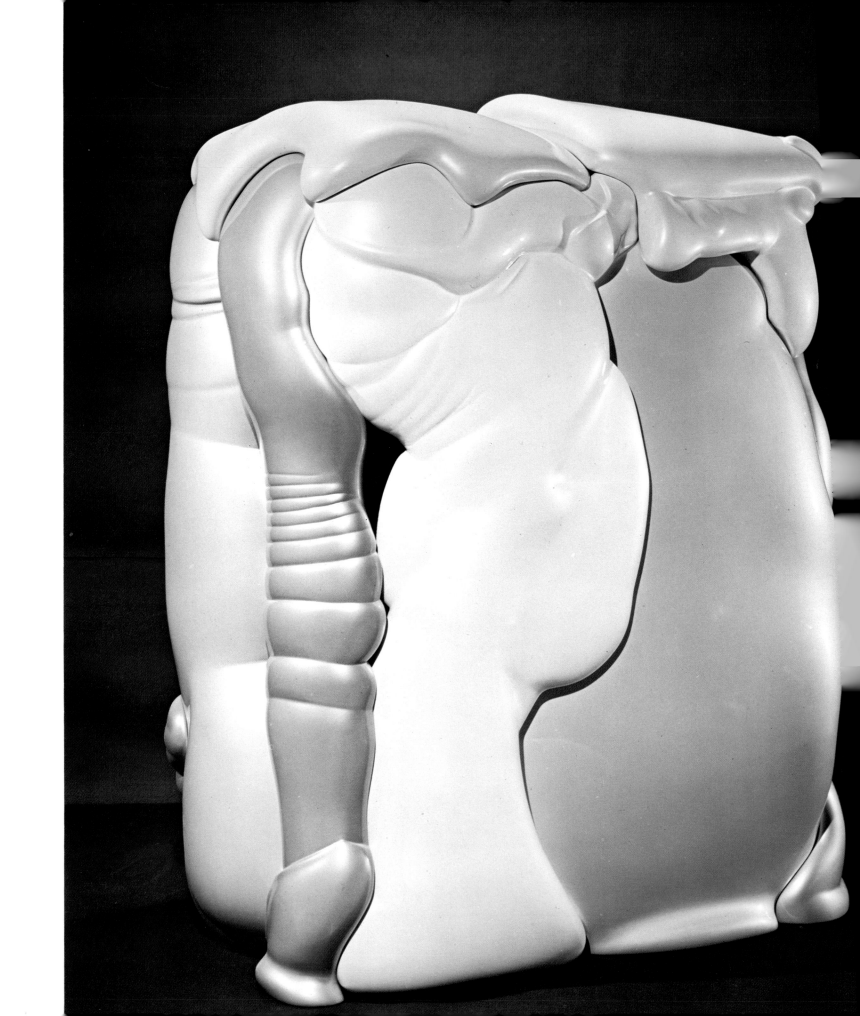

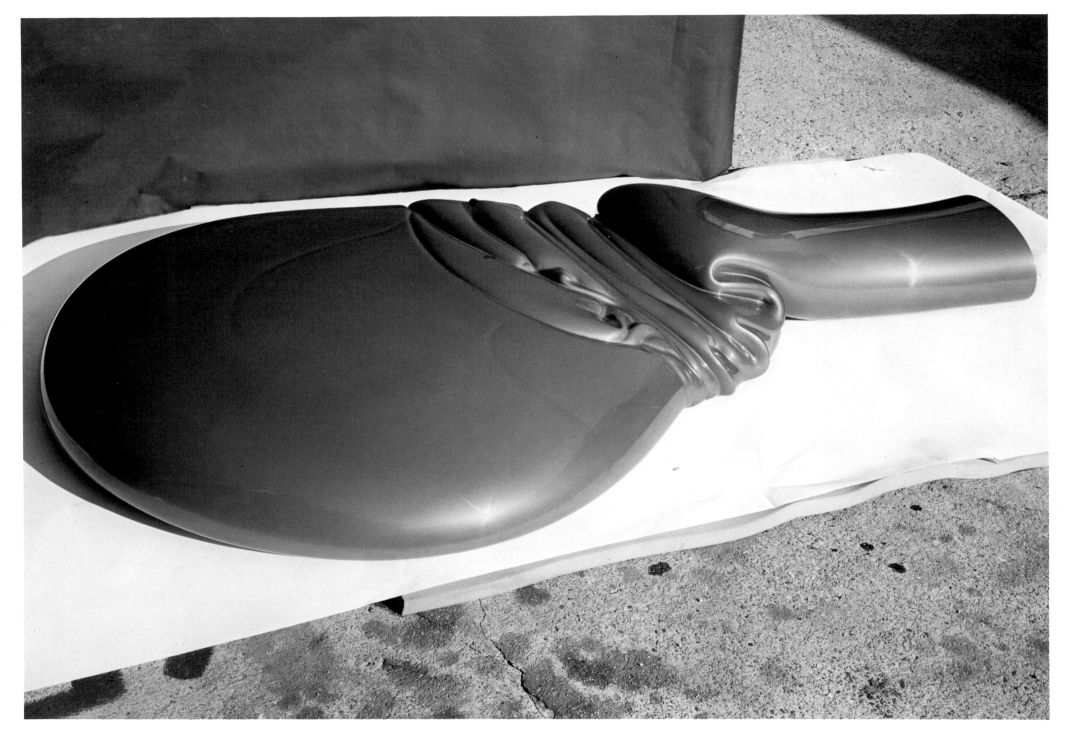

◄ 126
Expansion nº 39
1970

127
Expansion nº 1
1970

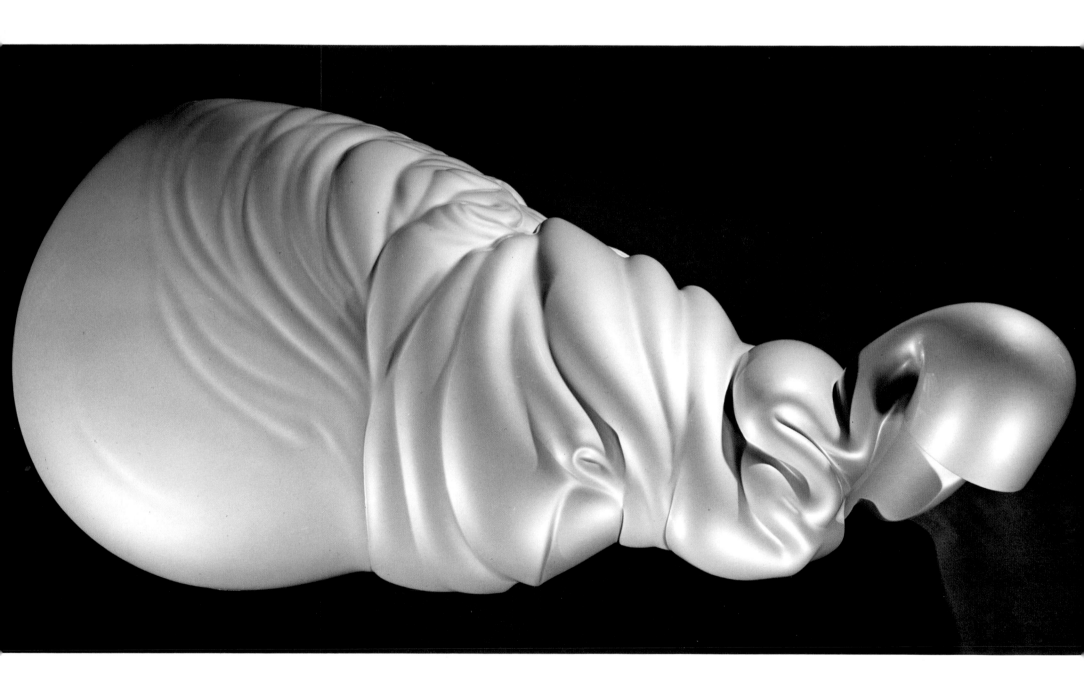

128
Expansion nº 6
1970

129 ▶
Expansion nº 5
1970

130
César avec *Expansion n° 15*, dans son atelier
de la rue Roger, Paris.
César with *Expansion No. 15*, in his studio
in the rue Roger, Paris
1970

a mountain of sensual flesh, a surface sensitized to the extreme. The third in this series of giants was a monumental steel fist designed to serve as the base for the mast in the courtyard of the military school of Saint-Cyr.

While *Thumb* was leading him back, more definitively, to his quantitative idiom, the year 1966 constituted for César a true balance sheet of his career: three large retrospectives were held at the Stedelijk Museum in Amsterdam, the Wilhelm-Lehmbruck-Museum der Stadt Duisburg, Germany, and at the Musée Cantini in his native city, Marseilles. Several one-man shows—also clearly retrospective in nature—in Turin, Rome, and Cannes, prompted him to finish the last metal sculptures left in his workshop, the *Postella* and *La Pacholette*.

Despite all the satisfaction that he was able to derive from this kind of official recognition, César remained eager for technical experimentation. The world of plastic materials fascinated him. Chemical engineers replaced the lathe operators, scrap-iron dealers, and arc welders of his former acquaintance. His experimental research on the casting of plastic was so much more costly that it could not be immediately financed. At last he found a sponsor, his old friend Marcel Lefranc, who would replace César's former dealers and eventually become both his backer and his agent.

At the beginning of 1967, in the forge/workshop of the owner of the Bateaux-Mouches, he discovered, by chance, the miracle substance polyurethane while trying to make castings with a synthetic foam with which he was unfamiliar. This substance, instead of conforming to the matrix of the mold, spread out into an astonishing organic form and congealed in a flexible and foamy mound that aroused his immediate enthusiasm.

The particular virtue of polyurethane consists of its ability to expand. It is a liquid mixture of polyester resin and of isocyanates that upon contact with the accelerating element, Freon, rapidly undergoes a reaction; the resulting "soft form" increases in volume by considerable proportions as compared with the initial quantity of the materials. To color the foam, one need only add the pigment of one's choice to the initial mixture. In a word, a quart of liquid resin crystallizes almost instantly into a mountain of solid foam. César was—one would imagine—particularly sensitive to the metamorphic power of the chemical reaction, and to the beauty of the result: a free form that expands organically in space, and derives its strange beauty from its own freedom of development. The flow of polyurethane is indeed neither preconceived nor delineated in advance; it is the pure and simple—and inevitable—result of a chemical reaction.

Once again César chose the Salon de Mai as the showroom for his exploits. He awed the Salon of 1967 with his new discovery, which expanded by eighty-eight quarts: the foam—an orange flow—swelled to some five yards in length, to the dimensions of a whale washed up on the beach. It struck us like a force of nature, a cataclysm. As usual, César managed to have me witness the operation, in a studio that he had rented especially for the purpose, in the rue Lhomond in the Latin Quarter. The ex-factory worker had become like a sorcerer's apprentice in a laboratory, only he worked at home. I participated in the collective euphoria, and the discovery took my breath away. The *homo ludens* surfaced immediately—César wanted to have the public participate in this spontaneous creation of free form. Thus, between 1967 and 1970, he organized a series of Happenings at the end of which the spectators were invited to cut up the expanded mass and to distribute the pieces like slices of a gigantic birthday cake. His public *Expansions* were conducted from Brussels to Rome and Genoa; from The Tate Gallery to the Fondation Maeght; from Lund, Göteborg, and Munich, to Rio de Janeiro and Montevideo. The last public performance took place in the very heart of Milan—in the center of the Galleria Vittorio Emanuele II—on November 28, 1970, in celebration of the anniversary of New Realism.

Everywhere, the ritual was the same: preparation of the resins, their mixture, the addition of colored pigment, the action of the Freon. The soft form, still sticky and fluid, overflowed the receptacles like an immense soufflé. César, helped by an assistant, spread the flow over the floor, which had previously been covered by a plastic sheet. It continued to spread, to increase in volume for several minutes. When the foam was practically dry it attained its maximum degree of expansion and its growth ceased—it had found its form. It was then that the scramble began. César attacked the *Expansion* and distributed the first pieces. The public, up until then sufficiently reserved, went wild, smashing, breaking, and then vying for scraps of this chemical feast which they gave to the Master to sign—"the last symptoms of a fetishism in the process of disappearing," as François Pluchart remarked.

For more than two years, I traveled with César. He had become the pioneer and apostle of this process of technological metamorphosis, and everywhere he staged the activity it ended in the euphoria of collective festivity. The ladies of London, the Bavarian guests of Gunther Sachs, and the habitués of Paris gallery openings reacted in as spontaneous and frenetic a fashion as the Belgian, Swedish, or Italian students, or the young Brazilian artists at the museum in Rio.

This ritual feast clearly corresponds to César's extroverted behavior. But at the root of these spectacles, or Happenings, there was the desire to make public a certain evolution of his artistic idiom. The artist intended, in that way, to give priority to the language of the material in the most orthodox appropriative gesture of New Realist art. In so doing, he achieved by his *Expansions* the exact theoretical counterpart of the *Compressions* and launched the second creative phase of this mechanical quantitative idiom. The *Expansions* are to plastic what the *Compressions* are to metal: underlying this new aspect of César's quantitative idiom we find the same fundamental grandeur based on the simplicity of the phenomena. The forms resulting from the expansion of polyurethane are beautiful, as are the *Compressions*, because they are the products of a technological process that has run its normal course, and because they are themselves.

By personally demonstrating this phenomenon of quantitative expression in its pure form, César conquered the public and forestalled scandal. The spectators, in many parts of the world, had the feeling of participating in the festivities, and also of understanding better the profound motivations of the artist. César reunites positively the collective sensibility of his time; he embodies its structural changes through a process of technological metamorphosis and he acts simultaneously to reveal this modernity. The spectators had the feeling of participating in a ritual of modern expressivity, of finding themselves on the threshold of the unlimited possibility of language. This fundamental harmony of communication between artist and public is essential. Now that the chemistry of plastics is in full development, with certain recently discovered products available commercially, it is of great importance that a sculptor has made us aware of the expressive possibilities of this new material. By such gestures, man affirms his presence in the midst of scientific progress. The legitimate hopes of our planet are based on the permanence of this technological humanism. When we remember that it was not until more than one hundred and fifty years after the advent of the first Industrial Revolution—founded on coal and iron—that the technology of a material so well known in society and so readily available found in González its first modern demiurge, César's immediate intervention in the still-experimental field of the chemistry of plastics takes on its full importance. Our visual world is conditioned today by this drastic reduction of the gap between the rhythm of technical progress and the appropriative range of the creative imagination. Contemporary sculpture, by concerning itself with the meeting between art and technology, tackles the problem on its proper level, by means of "collaboration" —as Yves Klein said—of intuitive communication, or rather through a shared humanism between the artist and the engineer. Of course, the undertaking is a long-term one, and we are seeing only the first advances. The truly human difficulties encountered in New York by E.A.T. (Experiments in Art and Technology) or by Maurice Tuchman in the realization of his "Art and Technology" program at the Los Angeles County Museum of Art are simultaneously indicative of our possibilities and our present limitations. But we are irremediably committed to the process. All over the world, moreover, individual and collective efforts of the same kind are springing up, conceived in the same initial terms and subject to the same difficulties. The advent of this worldwide awareness takes place at the cost of a collective change in modern sensibility—the shocks, renunciations, misunderstandings, and recantations that today still obstruct our vision tomorrow will be quickly forgotten.

The initial difficulties encountered by César in his experiments with plastic materials are today overlooked—seeming facility is the formidable privilege of artist/technologists. Everything appears to be easy: the technique does the work for them. But all was far from easy for César in 1967. One does not enter a chemistry laboratory as though it were a hardware factory—there is no small corner reserved for the artist to putter around in while other people are doing serious things. The chemists give you advice, and then the factories deliver their products to you. But you must manage for yourself—perhaps with the help of a technician—to concoct your mixtures wherever you can, creating all the acrid and noxious odors of chemical reactions that will undoubtedly arouse the anger of your neighbors. It took three years for César to overcome these difficulties. His new studio in the rue Roger in Montparnasse was perfectly equipped for the production of the monumental *Expansions* that were exhibited at the C.N.A.C. (Centre National d'Art Contemporain) in May, 1970, and that constituted the major attraction of the Paris season.

In 1967, César had not yet perfected his system of production or the brilliant and complex technique which gives the nonephemeral *Expansions* their pearly luster and their virtually unlimited resistance to wear and tear. He was preoccupied mostly with exploiting all the intrinsic possibilities of the material: the hard or soft foams, the different surface "skins." Those *Expansions* that were not destroyed were covered by César with a film of liquid polyester. There, again, the problem arose of the artist's intervention during the process of development of the form—the perpetual shifting from *homo faber* to *homo ludens*. The controlled *Expansions* of 1967 play on one of the properties of polyurethane: the superimposed flows blend together organically. Quantitative retouching is allowed. The most characteristic and monumental of these controlled *Expansions* suggests the prismatic form of the first automobile *Compressions*. On a prism of compressed plastic about six feet high various polychrome flows were distributed. The foam, in congealing on the sides of the prism, created different surface effects that correspond to the variations in frontality of the works in metal. César's creative imagination was once again operating according to its classical patterns.

This controlled *Expansion* was exhibited at the São Paulo Bienal of 1967 in a room devoted to César's sculpture, the most important room in the French section. Michel Ragon had organized the French exhibition, which offered a true retrospective of the sculptor's work. Alongside these recent *Expansions* were the human "Imprints" and César's masterpiece of metal sculpture, *The Victory of Villetaneuse*. It was a classical presentation of great distinction, faithful to the retrospective spirit of César's previous exhibitions at various European museums in 1965 and 1966. Would the jury have been more strongly impressed by a coherent and homogeneous ensemble of recent works, all of them in plastic? In all international competitions judgment is relative, and one could go on talking endlessly on the subject. I arrived in São Paulo in the middle of the jury's deliberations. The press was quite favorable to César, perhaps too much so. His presence—viewed objectively—dominated the whole Bienal; it was a very average exhibition, except for the American contribution that voluntarily remained outside the competition. César did not win the Grand Prize that he had hoped for, and he refused the consolation prize that was offered to him—a reward designed to encourage the "young." This gesture—in appearance one of pride—was actually one of dignity, and pointed up the confusion of values and the relativity of prizes in international competitions. The culture crisis in May of 1968, the boycott of the Venice Biennale, and the subsequent development of that institution proved that César was right.

On returning to Paris, César continued to exploit the practical possibilities of polyurethane foam. Such possibilities are indeed great: for instance, an especially flexible variant of this foam is used in the manufacture of synthetic mattresses all over the world. In 1968, at the exhibition "The Contemporary Seat" at the Musée des Arts Décoratifs, he displayed the prototype of a sofa produced in the workshops of the Mobilier National. He also presented the ideal "seat": a cube of flexible foam in which each human body leaves its own impression, according to one's particular weight and volume. A related, more baroque achievement was his covering of objects in plastic: a Dodgem car, such as one finds in amusement parks, was sawed in two, covered with foam, and transformed into a mini-sofa.

This concept of *Envahissement*—the covering of objects—was not a new one for César. He had done it many times with metal, and the foam stimulated his imagination anew. Sometimes he covered with foam the same objects that he had covered with metal, as was the case with an ostrich egg—a Paris collector owns a "metallic" and a "plastic" version of this same assemblage. The results of this kind of symbiosis are eminently baroque, or rather Art Nouveau. This is not surprising—César's taste, entirely shared by his wife, Rosine, is fixed on the Art Nouveau style that prevailed about 1900, on that aesthetic of soft forms which the use of plastics allowed him to introduce into his own work. In fact, the Baldaccini home in Paris, in the Villa Boulard—two steps from the mayor's office in the fourteenth arrondissement—with its green plants, its bizarre knickknacks, its mosaic fireplace, and its "covered" television, is a veritable museum of fin-de-siècle bric-a-brac.

César the decorator is inseparable from César the artist. He likes to recall that he made his debut in metal sculpture with a display of mattresses. His *Envahissements* in metal or plastic—from the large bootmaker's shoe to the television set or the ostrich egg—are displays of objects, more or less baroque commentaries designed to underscore the very heart of the subject: discourses in which the subject is the object. In July, 1971, at La Colombe d'Or in Saint-Paul-de-Vence, at César's friend Francis Roux's, I saw an old coffee grinder encased within sheets of compressed polyester: through the folds of the material, which suggested the pearly transparency of anisette, the object, intact and henceforth untouchable, was imbued with the sacred and hieratic quality of a cult

Continued on page 164

162

131.

132.

133.

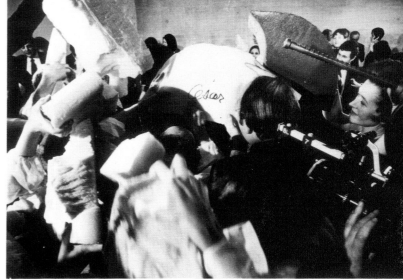

134.

131/136
Expansions réalisées en public
à la Tate Gallery, Londres.
Expansions created in public at
The Tate Gallery, London
1968

135. 136.

fetish. César the decorator is not simply a refined craftsman who welds andirons, or an amusing designer who casts armchairs in plastic, but a sensitive man who seeks to humanize the environment. The immense, flexible *Expansion* of some fifteen yards that he exhibited at the Milan Triennale of 1968 inspired an immediate feeling of well-being and comfort. Against the severity of the cement slab and support, this soft and soothing form induced relaxation and freedom of movement; it eliminated the sense of danger and aggressivity of the surroundings. On a more severe and refined formal plane, the long ribbon of foam (about twenty feet in length, ten in height, and fourteen inches wide) in the exhibition "Le Décor quotidien de la vie en 1968" ("Decoration in Daily Living in 1968"), at the Musée Galliera, played the same role—that of defining a moment of calm in space. I had organized this exhibition around the idea of a sense of nature, or if you prefer, a feeling for the environment, based on the worldwide growth of the industrial and urban phenomenon. The examples chosen—intended to illustrate the metamorphic appearance of modern life—had been defined within the limits and perspectives of the artistic idiom that they were attempting to free; their visual expressivity was thus in a state of conflict. The most obvious conflict embodied by all the pieces on exhibition had to do with the occupation of space. And César's solution—among the many references to the technical folklore of the object—was the most human, because it was the simplest.

While he pursued his research into the idiom of plastics, César was experimenting with the curiously parallel expressive possibilities of one of the noblest of traditional materials—crystal. Daum, an old glass factory in Lorraine that had produced Art Nouveau master-pieces by master glassblowers of the School of Nancy, asked César for permission to reproduce in glass one of his best-known *Envahisse-ments*—the half-broken ostrich egg from which a long plastic flow emerged. It was to be a multiple, to be mass-produced and sold in stores featuring glassware. The contract with César was part of a wider promotional scheme aimed at an imaginative revival of the glass industry. Daum solicited a number of other artists as well, including Salvador Dali and Leroy Neiman.

The collaboration between César and Daum did not end there. After the first multiple was finished, César offered to visit the Nancy factory before participating more directly in the creation of a second object. He was struck by the formal similarity of polyurethane paste and molten glass—the same compact liquidity, the same flow, the same brief working time. An idea immediately came to him—he would not re-create a pre-existing model, but would work the molten glass directly, in the light of his recent chemical experiments. The doors of the factory were opened to him. He charmed the glass-blowers of Lorraine as he had the scrap-iron dealers of Trans and Gennevilliers. During the winter of 1968 and the spring of 1969, he commuted between Paris and Nancy.

Broadening his technical knowledge little by little, César eventually evolved three principal methods of treating the material. The molten crystal balls weighing over forty pounds, wielded by the workers at the end of their glassblowing tubes, could be treated at a temperature of between 1,200 and 500 degrees centigrade, either in the form of an extended mass, a flat sheet, or a thin flow. Each choice determined a different formal procedure. Working with the mass or the flat sheet yielded flowing forms that approached the polyurethane *Expansions* in their freedom and inner dynamism. A thread of glass poured in a cubic graphite mold acquired, through crystallization, the look of accumulative blocks of glass "spaghetti" that suggested by their density César's metal *Compressions*. Color is imparted by subtle doses of traditional chemical coloring agents, especially lead oxides. The procedure is often delicate, and the most striking pieces remain the transparent ones, in which the material is allowed to speak for itself.

This collaboration between César and Daum resulted in the creation of some forty unique crystal sculptures, displayed at the Musée des Arts Décoratifs in October, 1969. The pieces were of unequal splendor—certainly decorative, as Jacques Michel, the critic of *Le Monde*, remarked—but stamped with the seal of their author's genius—strength, density, and freedom. The experiment also sanctioned an even more definite return to the Art Nouveau style, to which the material itself and its history easily lent themselves.

During 1969 and the first part of 1970, César turned to still better account the aesthetic properties of the soft forms that emerged from the polyurethane. Concerned with the survival of the forms as such—for the sake of the harmony of a particular smooth surface or molten cascade of loose folds—and with the immanence of their eventual flow, the sculptor, surrounded by a technical crew, perfected a complex process which made the *Expansions* of that period beautiful objects with a thoroughly reliable solidity. They were as light as aluminum or cork, as imputrescible as teakwood, as resistant as stone.

The polyurethane flows, which originally crumbled easily, were strengthened by a protective film, pumiced and given a high gloss. Their colors, increasingly subtle and contrasting with the lively tones of yellow-orange, raspberry red, and blue-green of the ephemeral public *Expansions*, were the result of a subtle addition of values and successive touches of glaze. They have, moreover, lent their names to the pieces exhibited in May, 1970, at the C.N.A.C.: *Black Pearl, Pale Pearl Mauve, Yellow Gold, Iridescent White*, among others. César succeeded in reconciling the needs for survival of the object with the organic freedom of its form: the mold and final casts scrupulously respect the order of the folds, the waves and undulations of the flow, and the sometimes chaotic phenomena of inner and outer tension of the material. The extreme refinement of the work heightens its spontaneity of form. This alliance between organic freedom in structure and remarkable precision in the treatment of the material gives the series of definitive *Expansions* of 1970 (classified under the generic term "plastics") a monumentality that is itself the mark of grandeur. Monumentality is certainly not solely a question of size, although most of the pieces in the series are six to nine feet in length and five feet wide. The smaller elements, as well as certain fragments of the *Expansions* (actual slices of larger works displayed on the wall like reliefs—one more example of the frontality of César's work), retain the same density of appearance, the same impact of their thrust into space. Another diverse approach consists in spreading the polyurethane on a flat support (such as a right angle, step, or the edge of a table). The final flow combines the unevenness of a relief and the irregularities of its contours. One of the most striking pieces in the series *(Black Pearl)* consists of a tubular and ringed flow, erected vertically and merging with a broad horizontal form. It suggests a cascade that is fixed in space, ready to defy the force of gravity, as in a film projected in reverse.

Since 1968, César has used numerous ephemeral *Expansions* as models for metal castings or reproductions in marble. The presence of these forms is so strong that their true nature is disguised: Carrara marble gives the illusion of plastic! There is, nevertheless, no comparison with the plastic sculpture series of 1970 that so effectively combined mastery of means with freedom of form. The Parisian public, generally so divided with regard to César, was united this time in its acclaim. His success has been total, without reservations.

Continued on page 217

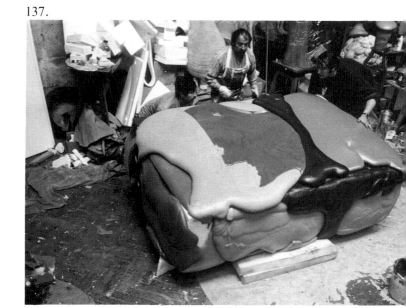

137.

137/138
César prépare des Expansions
dans son atelier de la rue Lhomond, Paris.
César creating Expansions in his
studio in the rue Lhomond, Paris
1967

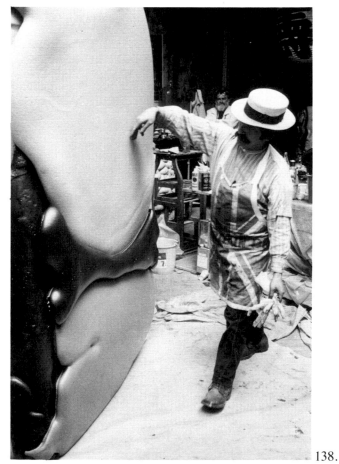

138.

139
Méridienne
Couch
1968

140 ▶
Expansion
1968

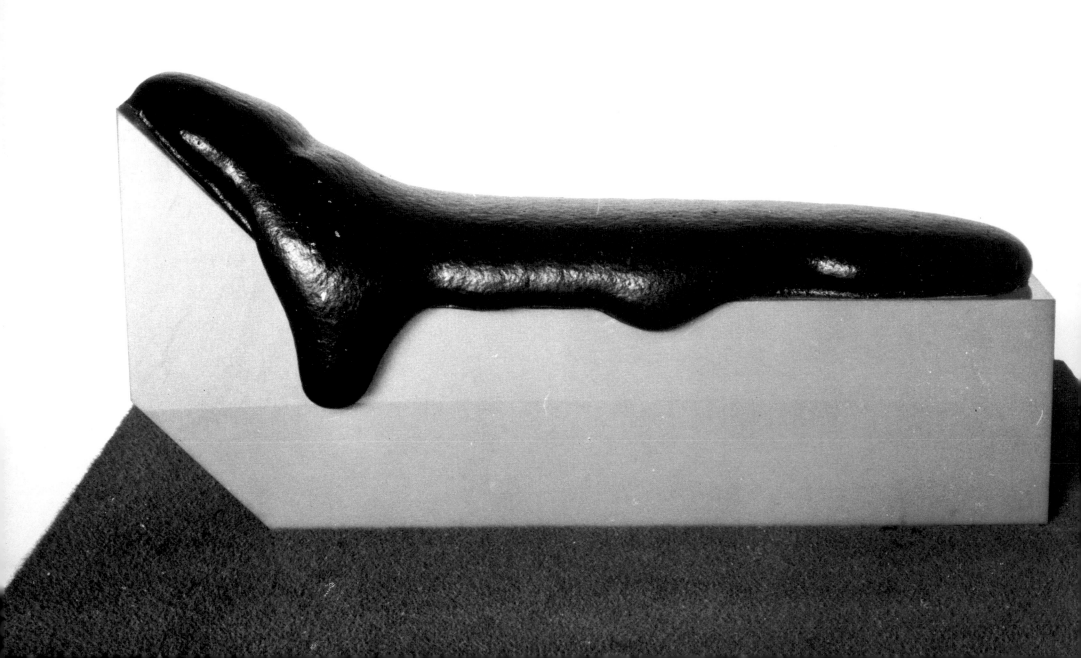

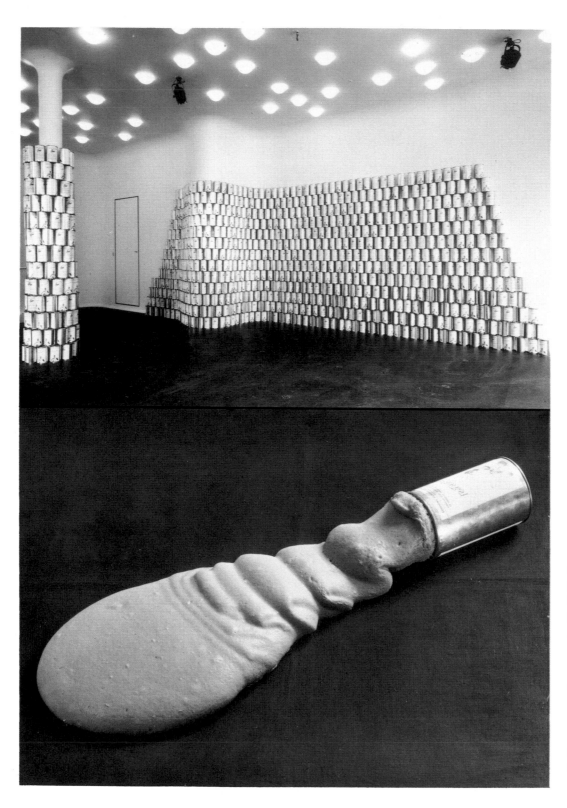

170

141
Conserve expansion
à la Galerie Givaudan, Paris.
Container Expansion
at Galerie Givaudan, Paris
1969

142
Coulée jaune
Yellow Flow
1969

143 ▶
Conserve expansion
Container Expansion
1969

172

144
Expansion nº 19
1970

145 ▶
Expansion
de Matignon
1970

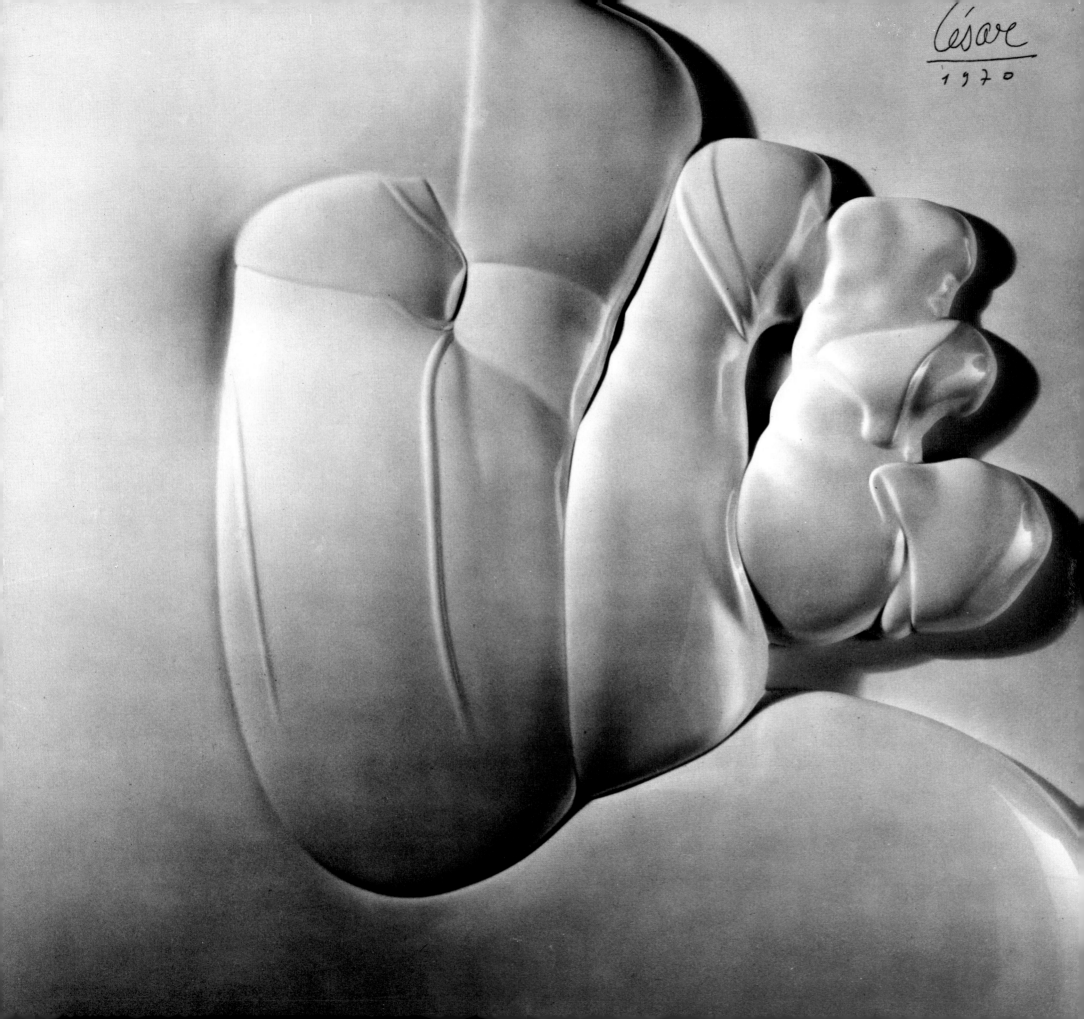

176

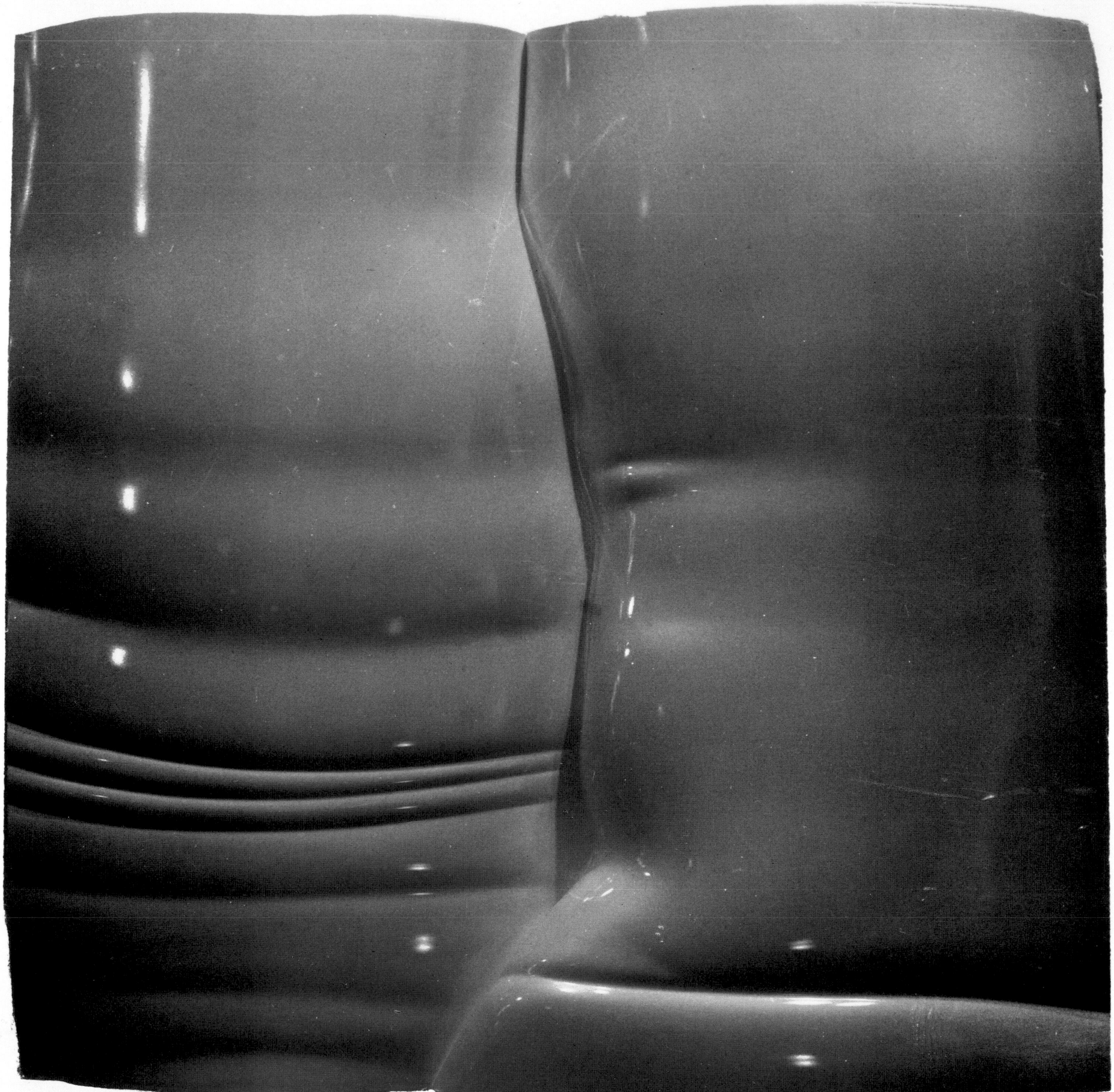

177

◄ 148
Expansion nº 18
1970

149
Expansion nº 27
1971

◄ 150
Expansion nº 51
1973

151
Expansion nº 34
1970

152
Compression plastique
1971

153 ▶
Compression
plastique
1971

◄ 154
Compression
plastique
1971

155
Compression
plastique
1971

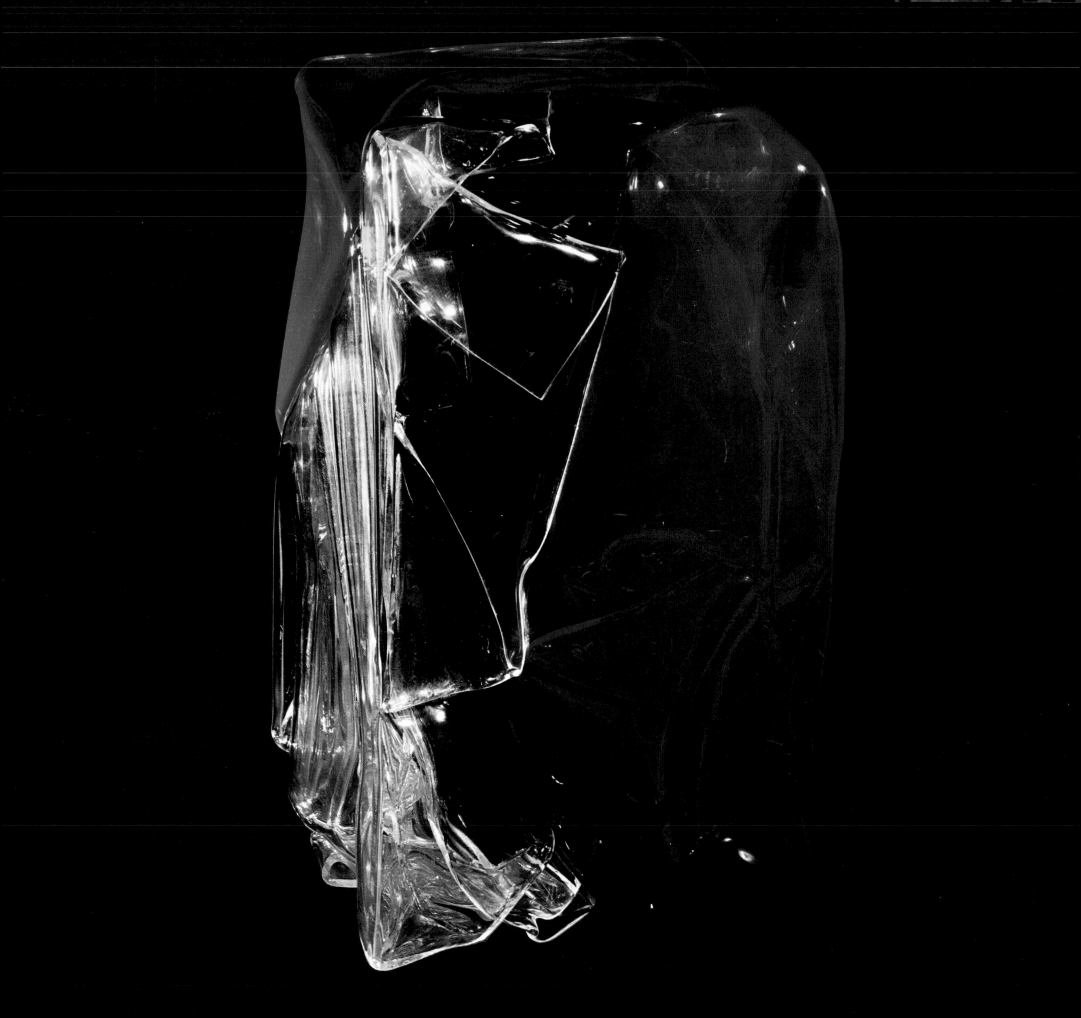

◄ 156
Compression plastique
1971

157
Compression plastique
1971

158 ▶
Compression plastique
1972

159
Compression plastique
1972

189

◄ 160
Objet enveloppé
Enclosed Object
1971

161
Objet enveloppé
Enclosed Object
1971

162/163
César au travail
dans les ateliers des
Cristalleries Daum.
César working at the Daum
crystal factory at Nancy
1969

164
César réalise une
Combustion d'allumettes,
Nice.
César creating
Burned Matches,
Nice
1971

162.

164.

166.

163.

165.

165
L'artiste à l'exposition « Tête à têtes »,
Galerie Creuzevault, Paris.
The artist at the « Tête à têtes » exhibition,
Galerie Creuzevault, Paris
1973

166
César à l'exposition « Formes libres », Galleria del Naviglio, Milan.
César at the «Free Forms» exhibition, Galleria del Naviglio, Milan
1970

167
César à l'exposition « César chez Daum »,
Musée des Arts Décoratifs, Paris.
César at the « César at Daum's » exhibition,
Musée des Arts Décoratifs, Paris
1969

167.

168
Cristal nº 89
1969

169
Cristal nº 63
1969

170 ▶
Cristal nº 93
1969

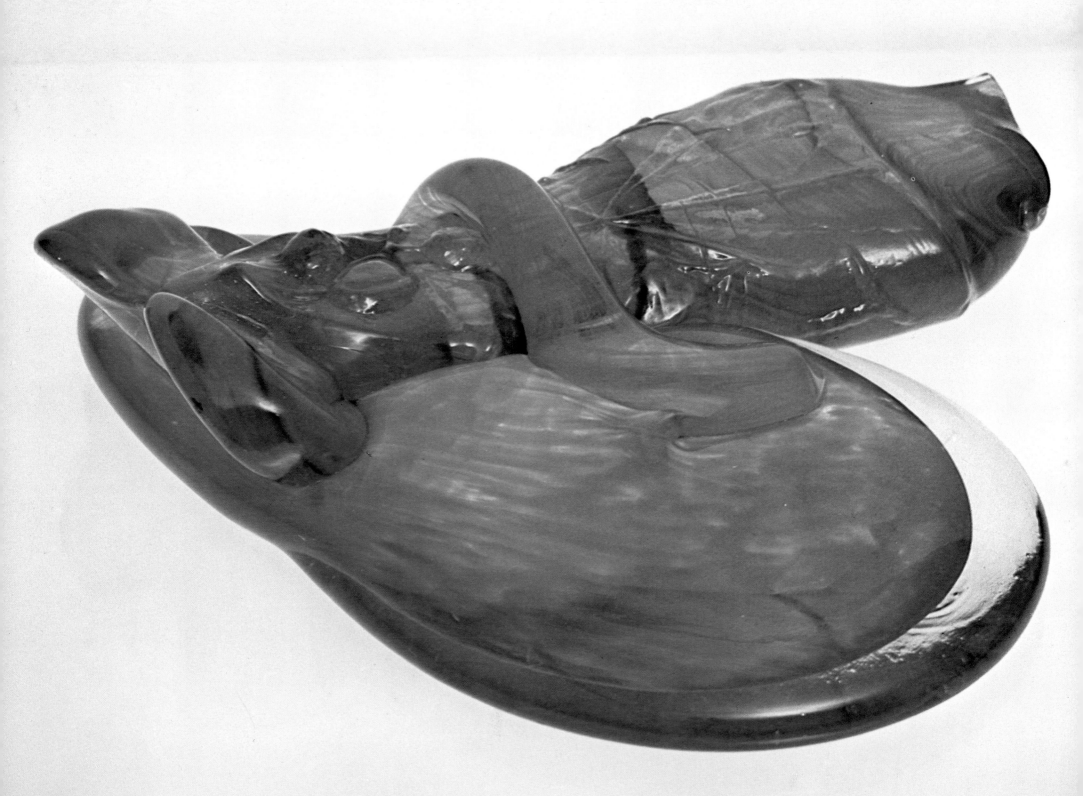

171
Cristal nº 16
1969

172 ►
Cristal nº 61
1969

◄ 173
Expansion
1967

174
Expansion murale
1970

175
Expansion Godet
Goblet Expansion
1969

176
Expansion Pinceau
Paintbrush Expansion
1969

177
Petite Pièce ronde
Small Round Object
1969

178 ▶
Œuf n° 2
Egg No. 2
1969

179
Footballeur,
objet compressé
Compressed Object:
Football Player
1970

180 ▶
Pendule,
objet compressé
Compressed Object:
Clock
1971

201

181
Objets compressés
Compressed Objects
1971

182 ▶
Objet compressé
Compressed Object
1971

205

◄ 183
Combustion
d'allumettes
Burned
Matches
1970

184
Combustion
d'allumettes
Burned
Matches
1971

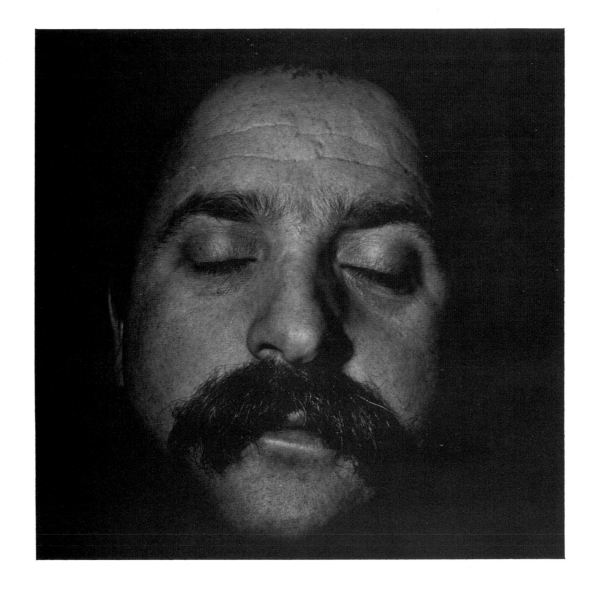

◄ 185
Tête romaine
Roman Head
1966

186
César s'est fait photographier
« en masque », 1960.
Dix ans plus tard, il réalisera les
Masques déformés.
Photograph of César wearing a mask, 1960
Ten years later, he created
the *Masques déformés*

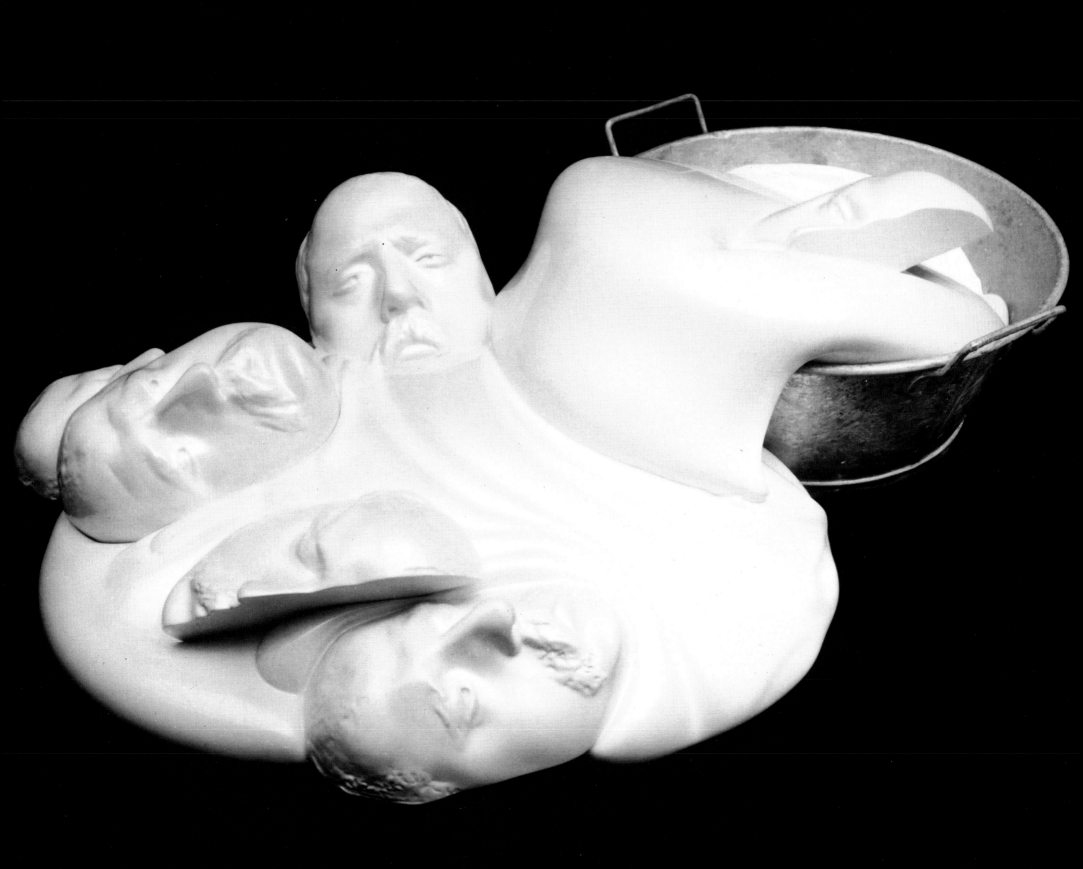

188
Masques déformés. Photographie de trois sérigraphies
par César, sur feuilles de plastique, déformées à la chaleur.
Distorted Masks. Photograph of three silk-screens by César,
printed on sheets of plastic, and distorted by heat
1970

210

189
« Tête en pain »
« Head in Bread »
(Bronze)
1973

190 ▶
« Tête en pain ».
(Pain)
« Head in Bread ».
(Bread)
1973

212

191
Masque nº 39
1972

192 ▶
Masque nº 31
1972

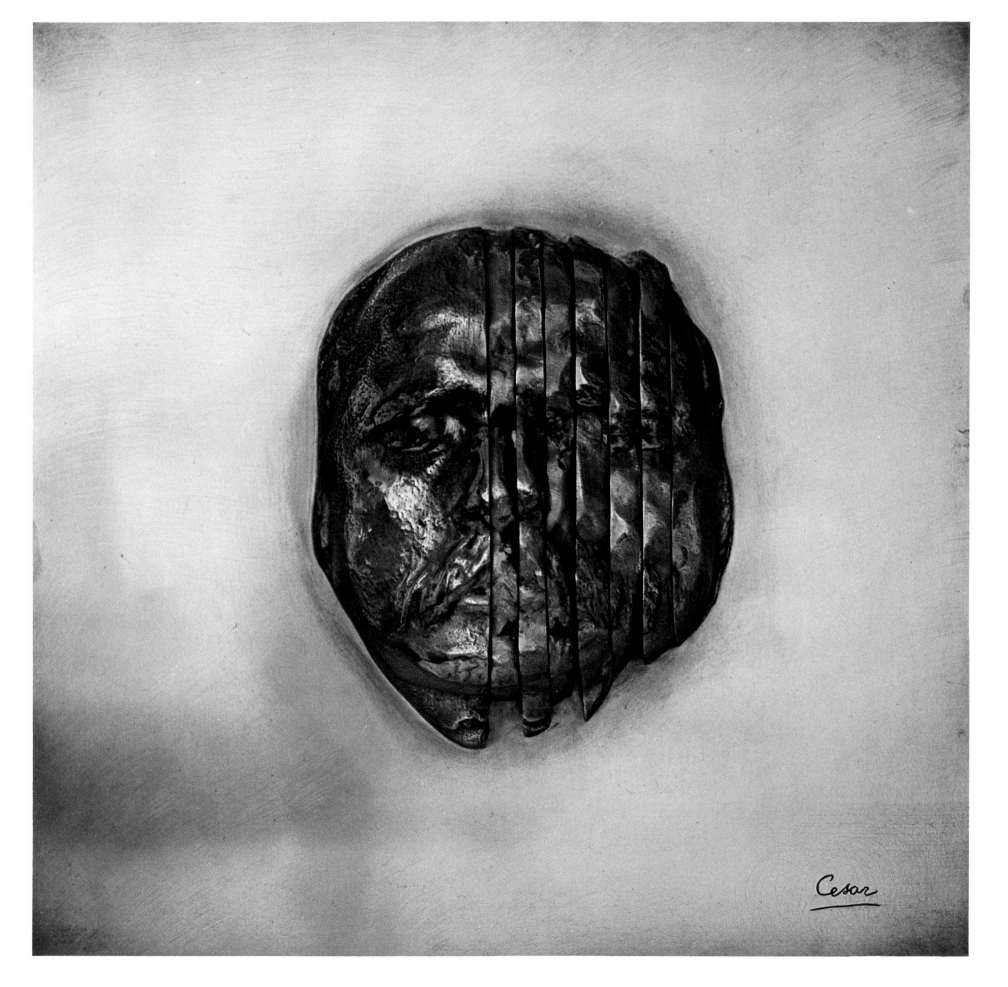

193
Bijoux compressés nº 116
Jewelry Compression No. 116
1972

194
Bijoux compressés nº 97
Jewelry Compression No. 97
1971

216

195
Compression
orfèvrerie 2 bis
Silverware
Compression 2a
1971

During the summer of 1970, César settled in the south of France, in Saint-Paul-de-Vence. He decided to buy a country house nearby, at Roquefort-les-Pins, and chose a former horse farm, where the stables could easily be converted into guest rooms.

With success, he seemed to lose interest in his *Expansions*, at least for the moment. In fact, incapable of resting on his laurels, he was as usual doing something else. His sculptures, because of their perfection, had become remote to him. What remained for him was the priority of appropriation, the mastery of technique, the paternity of style. He had proved himself, and had the feeling of having given what was expected of him, that is to say, perfect sculptures—something that for the moment was in abeyance but that he could and would resume again whenever he liked. After having intensely accepted the challenge of his artistic gift, he had assured its future by putting it aside—an attitude typical of César, of his innate desire to preserve the free play of his imagination, independent of this or that contingency. The C.N.A.C. exhibition traveled to many European cities during 1970 and 1971, including Brussels, Oslo, and Hamburg. Visitors to the openings witnessed the spectacle of César's surprising lack of concern about this important moment in his career.

In the company of a photographer from Nice named Ferrero, who served as a kind of honorary assistant to the artist, he made the rounds of the scrap-iron dealers of the Côte d'Azur and discovered a number of motorcycles, which he hastened to compress in their entirety—tires, seats, rearview mirrors, and headlights included. Unlike the automobile *Compressions*, where the basic element was the metal body, exclusively, the motorcycle *Compressions*, because of the variety of their elements and their behavior in the press, have a more anecdotal and dramatic appearance that is highly evocative of an accident. But in their fixed visceral state, they stress so peremptorily the suspension of time, the precise and fleeting instant of the paroxysm of a shock wave, that they can properly be called stupefying in their realism. Ten years after the

Compressions of the Salon de Mai, when one might have expected something less, César provided additional proof of his virtuosity. At the exhibition in 1970 at the Galleria Schwarz in Milan, the motorcycle *Compressions* were a dazzling success but hardly a surprise to those who in 1969 had seen the retrospective exhibition of small classical *Compressions* (works of 1961, 1963, 1968–69) at the Galerie Mathias Fels in Paris.

At the same time, César was doing mini-*Compressions* of toys and everyday objects on wooden panels. The *Compressions* of miniature racing cars and motorcycles are charged with healthy, forthright humor. The mini-*Compressions* of objects such as kitchen utensils and cameras, although they have a certain plastic interest, pose a problem that might well be termed—within the appropriative perspective of New Realism—a conflict of scope, a limiting of the artistic idiom that Arman also shares. The Arman of the *Colères* —broken, twisted, shattered, and burned objects—is sometimes close to the César of the mini-*Compressions*. The creator of the *Petit Déjeuner sur l'herbe* of 1957 has the moral right to compress any object he likes. It makes no difference that Arman's quantitative idiom hinges on the notion of breakage, in a sense the dialectical counterpart of the notion of accumulation. Arman is a man with a single, though two-sided idea, positive and negative, the center of energy of a magnetic field at once precise and limited. His work is based on the pure and simple appropriation of the object and not on the mastery of this or that material, the conquest of this or that technique. Arman is an introvert who defends his territory. When the *homo ludens* in César prevails over the *homo faber*, his imagination no longer recognizes frontiers. This conflict of abilities led to a conflict of personalities—not a serious matter between artists.

Even in the minor genres, César remains consistent, seizing upon one of the focal points of his work, one of the nuclei of his imagination, as his point of departure. The *Portraits* of 1969 are a carry-over of the "Imprints." One such work is a transfer onto plastic of a photo-portrait of César by Rotella. Another is an "Imprint" in relief of César's facial mask. All of them are heat-treated, then swollen, distended, and deformed by the blows of a blunt instrument.

After experimenting with this type of visual humor (elsewhere, as well, with the flat image, in the "controlled" photogravure), César determined to systematize the process of objectification. From a cast of his face he made a series of multiples in the form of embossed plastic plaques. By exposing the reliefs to heat, he obtained innumerable extensions, distortions, and combinations. He chose among this rich collection of distorted forms the definitive "heads" to be cast in bronze. The original head served as the model for a cast in bread. The round "César-loaves" made by the master baker Poilane were cut up during the opening of "Tête à Têtes" at the Galerie Creuzevault in March, 1973. The exhibition reassembled in three clearly differentiated stages of the material—plastic, bronze, and bread—fragments of César's face, torn or bruised, obtuse or obese, laughing or sardonic. It was a veritable narcissistic frieze in high relief, totally striking in its expressive vitality.

This exhibition, whose content seemed minimal at first, gradually became enriched as a result of our conversations. It made me realize how much César, in 1973, was once again troubled by the recurring problem of "métier," of the direct intervention of the artist in the language of art, of his effective control of all the resources brought into play, and his responsibility toward the entire process of elaboration. By initiating a return to the figure, in every sense of the word, the "Tête à Têtes" exhibition marked a stepping stone in the future evolution of César's art.

Another minor genre, the compositions of matchboxes burned and glued to a flat surface, constitutes a complicated synthesis of multiple references to the three former attempts in paper sculpture from before 1948, the repetitive cadences of the *Plaques*, the *Boxes*, and finally the collage/drawings of 1961.

What, on the other hand, is in no way minor was his return to the problem of compression; he sought to integrate all the basic elements of the object being compressed, to go beyond the purely metallic stage. Already in his 1970 "light" *Compressions* of imprinted aluminum tubes (from household and pharmaceutical products), the colors and impressions produced a heterogeneous image, and created both a mental and visual distance with respect to the metal. The *Compressions* of complete motorcycles introduced the dimension of time into the idiom of quantitative appropriation. The shock wave is embodied in the precise moment of traumatism. The pivot of communication consequently shifts—it is no longer so much the new stage of the metal itself to which we react, but rather to the notion of shock that is implied. We become, in a way, the witnesses of an extreme condition in the history of the object. In November, 1970, at the historical exhibition that I organized at the Galleria Rotonda della Besana in Milan on the occasion of the anniversary celebration of New Realism, César displayed a flat *Compression*—an automobile completely squashed from top to bottom. The height of the vehicle was reduced to less than two feet. This "pancake" of scrap-metal, affixed to a supporting wall and displayed vertically, could have been considered the culmination, in some way the final stage of César's series of automobile-body reliefs. But displayed as it was, on the ground, its meaning was quite different. The work had the virtue of a testimony, for it preserved the signs of its compression; its effect on the public was thus all the more fascinating since it bore evidence of the violence it had suffered. The purely metallic *Compression* embodies the aesthetic fact of passage to a higher stage of the metal. We are sensitive to effects of burning, bursting, or twisting as expressive elements of a technical idiom of quantitative appropriation—we react to a metallic *Compression* as to a sculpture. This, moreover, is what its creator hoped for, by assuming the moral responsibility for his act of appropriation and its result.

The compression of an object in its entirety represents, in a way, an act of revenge on the metal.[7] In a total compression, the diverse mixture of elements—such as leather, rubber, fabric, glass, and Plexiglas—that are part of the object being compressed undergo varying reactions during the process. The different situations of expressivity that result contrast with the absolute homogeneity and perfect visual coherence of the metal *Compressions*. We are in the presence of a new image, one that bears witness to the inner history of the object. It is no longer the metal that speaks to us, but the object itself that shows us what has happened to it. Our vision is then automatically colored by emotion—tension turns into violence, our technical folklore is altered, and, for the artist, communication through the quantitative idiom is in the form of repression not expression.

Technology thus becomes controversial, or, to be more exact, self-critical. The *Compressions* of entire motorcycles—like the flattened automobile—are to the history of sculpture what Jean-Luc Godard's film *Week-end* is to the history of cinema. The conflict is obvious between the structural treatment of the material—which constitutes a problem with regard to the artistic idiom on the part of the sculptor—and the subsequent bursting forth of an image that attests to the repressive violence to which the object was subjected and poses a sociopolitical problem, a problem of conscience.

The theoretical and logical solution of the conflict lies in political commitment. César is incapable of programming his vision in terms of theoretical imperatives or objectives. Others work by theory, he works by instinct. In art, his instinct carries him toward New Realism; in politics, it carries him toward the Left. It is easy to foresee that he will continue to involve himself, honestly, in numerous conflicting situations, without pretending to save appearances by so-called logical behavior. Can one, moreover, conceive of César not permanently in a conflict of conscience? There are not two Césars. The supporter of Fidel Castro and the supporter of General de Gaulle are one and the same unique person—a person in perpetual conflict with himself, with his *homo faber* and *homo ludens*, but a complete person, whose profound integrity is indestructible. Beyond every contradiction, César remains César. The secret of his being? A true intellectual love of freedom—freedom conceived as the supreme value of an awareness of existence, art being only the existential manifestation of that freedom. Freedom to dream and, if possible, to realize one's dreams—this is where art comes in, following eternally in the wake of the imagination. Far be it from me to try to make a hero of César, and to find a comfortable philosophical justification for the real or apparent contradictions of his nature. But I think I know the man and his work well enough to bear witness to both. César is the man of every compromise, but only up to a certain point, a certain impassable limit. And this limit appears when César feels what he calls his "reality"—the full use of freedom—being threatened. Any hindrance to the imagination constitutes the gravest offense against the spirit, since the smallest restraint can block the delicate functioning of this mental "laboratory" in which a poetic vision of the world is ceaselessly being elaborated.

Superficial appearances are often against César. Why did he continue to practice welded metal sculpture up until 1966, or six years after his *Compressions* and one year after *Thumb*? Why did he resume his *Compressions* in 1968, after a lapse of five years, three years after the human "Imprints," one year after the *Expansions*? In both cases, César's answers are identical: "Since I knew how to do figures before, why shouldn't I make them as well later on? The Compressions were my own idea; I've assumed their paternity and made them my own style." And in a similar manner he claims credit for the *Expansions*.

César's only capital is his imagination, and the talent that is at its service. This capital was won at great cost, and he does not intend to lose a single piece of it. Moreover, he puts it to the best use. The results speak for themselves: *The Victory of Villetaneuse* (1965) is a masterpiece that lifts metal sculpture to a level unmatched by any work prior to 1960; the integral *Compressions* of 1970 evoke the quantitative aesthetic of those first "bales" of 1960; after the ephemeral *Expansions* of 1967—pure examples of César's artistic idiom—he conferred true nobility on polyurethane with his series of monumental plastic sculptures of 1970.

In 1971, parallel with experiments as numerous as they were varied, César produced a true synthesis of style—the *Compression*—and of treatment of the material—plastic. The *Compressions* of plastic materials, of 1971, suggest the traditional form of the metal "bales"; they are the result of the compression of sheets of polyester crumpled under heat. The process allows infinite variations in form as well as in color, from absolute transparency to fluorescent effects at the edges. The plastic *Compression* assumed baroque forms with the greatest naturalness, the obvious consequence of the extreme flexibility of the basic material. César used the crumpled and transparent sheets to envelop objects, such as a typewriter, electric fan, and coffee grinder, and again recaptured the spirit of his *Envahissements*. Finally, the plastic material allows for work in a broad range of sizes—from the monumental *Compression* to the mini-object that can be produced as a multiple. The process, the result of various experiments, henceforth assumes the dimensions of a discursive panorama, a true presentation of the sculptor's repertory. It is rather significant, also, that César should have chosen the Galerie Lucien Durand, the site of his first Paris exhibition in 1954, for his 1972 show of plastic *Compressions*.

If the liberties one takes are justified by the uses to which they are put, then César is not beholden to anyone. And this is what he says himself, without beating around the bush, when he feels that he has made further advances in his work. "It's what I do that counts. If I do it, it's because I feel the need, and there's no reason for me to justify myself," he stated in 1965, after displaying *Thumb* at the Galerie Claude Bernard. If he defies public incomprehension, it is because he knows that he has revitalized art with his mechanical quantitative idiom, thus pointing the way to the future. "I understood what the public was waiting for—not for me to become a personality, but for my sculptures," he declared in Marseilles in 1966 when his native city gave him the homage he was due: forty sculptures from 1954–66 were exhibited at the Musée Cantini, under the sponsorship of the mayor, Gaston Defferre. Apart from any sentimental satisfaction, César noted that his *Compressions* and human "Imprints" held their own beside his classical metal sculptures, and he was ready to go forward: "A show like the one at the Musée Cantini puts everything in place." And indeed, a few months later he began a new chapter in his work—the *Expansions*—with the great orange flow exhibited at the Salon de Mai.

Habit certainly becomes second nature. But to place oneself permanently in a controversial situation is not always so simple or so comfortable. Often the conflict degenerates into a deadlock. Since 1967, César had been in close touch with Claude Renard, who had originated a project called "Art et Industrie" at the Renault Company. This was a promotional program that placed interested artists in direct contact with industry and put at their disposal the production equipment of a large firm. It was up to the artists to choose whatever elements they felt were best suited to express themselves, from the extremely wide range of this technical repertory. Arman initiated a series of exhibitions that resulted from this collaboration between art and industry, and he was closely followed by Alain Jacquet, Jean-Pierre Raynaud, and Sanejouand, among others. Arman had no difficulty in tackling the Renault problem. His quantitative style—cuttings of motors, accumulations of spare parts—lent itself marvelously to the operation. César's first reaction was predictable: he proposed to compress, model by model, the entire line of automobiles produced by the Renault factories. Claude Renard's objection was likewise predictable: the compression of an entire object dramatizes the image and embodies the myth of the accident. In vain, César tried to demystify the idea of violence by decking it out in borrowed plumes. He imagined having the vehicles smashed up by stunt drivers, and then restoring the automobiles' initial splendor—the brilliance of their paint and chrome surfaces— while preserving the structural alterations to the body and frame caused by the impact of the crash. To put it plainly, to repaint and return to a state of newness a crumpled-up automobile. The idea was superbly baroque and spectacular, but can one really overcome the danger of repressive violence by displaying an excess of humor? This second idea abandoned, César turned to a sure position, to a classical element in his repertoire, the *Envahissement* of the object. An automobile door covered by polyurethane foam is held in a vertical position by the mass of foam that serves as its base. This process of *Envahissement* clearly could have resolved the question since it offered an extremely diversified range of objective possibilities. The solution was aesthetically elegant but it constituted a half measure, and I doubt that César has ever been really satisfied with it. Matters dragged on, and a complete impasse was reached. On the one hand, the artist had not succeeded in making the purest and simplest solution—that is to say, the reality of his style—prevail, but on the other hand, he was anxious not to let this unique opportunity to become involved in the industrial folklore of his time escape him. César has no desire to overlook such technical challenges, for they always serve as stimulants to his imagination. One day everything will clear up, either because he will have renounced the problem in its entirety by finding a totally satisfying original solution, or because he will have accepted the intermediate solution, having found something else somewhere else!

At this stage of the analysis, one begins to think that the moral problems of César are shared by all men today, living in the same industrial civilization and subject, at all levels, to some form of repressive intervention by society. The essence of César's genius lies, perhaps, in making us forget that he is great, by showing himself a human among humans.

But in such a case it is as pointless to separate the man from his work as it is the work from the man. The son of an Italian cooper from Marseilles possessed the necessary talent, will, and flexibility to succeed. Life has not spared him from hardships or obstacles. He always had to struggle in order to satisfy his need to create; the rift remains constant between his ego and his reality—poverty first, and afterward fame. The underlying fabric of his existence doomed him to anonymity. Not only did he know how to preserve his talent—formed in the harsh school of tradition—but he has developed, heightened, and expanded it in the midst of the extraordinary changes in the sensibility of his time. The most classical of metal sculptors is the most modern plunderer of industrial folklore; the most skillful craftsman is the most adventurous seeker.

That César should have focused his intuition on contemporary life, that he has made us see it with new eyes through some of the most poetic fragments of his oeuvre, that he arrived at the essence of his artistic idiom by employing elements produced by modern technology—this is the chain of events that has assured the sculptor his true place in the contemporary art world, simultaneously in the midst of and yet beyond the New Realism of Europe. And César will remain one of its most original protagonists. His work has exceeded the specific framework of the individual venture and has taken its place in the evolution of contemporary sculpture. Born, trained, and recognized in a period subject to a residual past, he dared at a crucial moment in his career to question an entire hierarchy of values. And instead of letting himself be carried away by the shipwreck of a dead culture, he stamped the new sensibility with a seal that is all the more indelible because it represents both the personality of the artist and his work. César's place is among the great.

196
César dirige la compression
d'un objet à Nice.
César directing the compression
of an object in Nice
1971

197
César dirige la compression
d'une motocyclette à Nice.
César directing a motorcycle
compression in Nice
1971

196.

197.

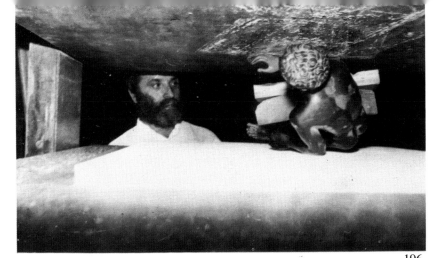

198.

199.

200.

198
César, avec la même motocyclette
compressée, à Nice.
César with the same motorcycle
compression, in Nice
1971

199
César dans l'atelier d'orfèvrerie à Nice.
César in a goldsmith's atelier in Nice
1972

200/201
César dans sa maison de campagne
de Roquefort-les-Pins.
César in his country house
in Roquefort-les-Pins
1973

201.

NOTES

1. Michel Ragon, "César sculpteur de l'âge industriel," *Jardin des Arts*, No. 154, September, 1967.

2. Alain Jouffroy, "Qui est César," *Opus International*, No. 17, April, 1970.

3. Douglas Cooper, *César*. Vol. 9 in the "Artistes de notre temps" series. Amriswil, Switzerland: Bodensee-Verlag, 1960.

4. After an initial manifesto published on April 16 in Milan, Pierre Restany founded the New Realists group in Paris, at the home of Yves Klein, on October 27, 1960, in the presence of Arman, François Dufrêne, Raymond Hains, Klein, Martial Raysse, Daniel Spoerri, Jean Tinguely, and Jacques de la Villeglé. César and Mimmo Rotella were absent, though invited. They took part in later manifestations of the group, which was soon joined by Niki de Saint-Phalle in 1961 and by Christo and Deschamps in 1962. The collective activities of the New Realists, chiefly centered around the Galerie "J" in Paris, extended over three years (1960–63) and were marked —in addition to the group's participation in many salons and biennials— by two festivals (Nice, 1961; Munich, 1963) and numerous individual shows. Beginning in 1964, various museums devoted exhibitions to the New Realists. In 1968, Pierre Restany's book *Les Nouveaux Réalistes*, which traces the history of the movement, was published by Éditions Planète in Paris. In November, 1970, a festival celebrating the tenth anniversary of the founding of the group took place in Milan, at the Galleria Rotonda della Besana and in the historic center of the city.

5. Daniel Abadie, "César et la révolution du matériau," *Études*, June, 1970.

6. Georges Boudaille, "Conversation autour d'un pouce avec César," *Les Lettres Françaises*, 30 December 1965.

7. Beginning in the summer of 1971, the formula applied to precious metals gave way to the production of mini-*Compressions* in gold and silver that constitute an important event in the history of the jeweler's art. The basic idea is the compression of everything offered—the entire contents of one's jewel box is emptied into César's hands. The result of the operation fixes forever, in the block of a mini-sculpture, the highlights of one's personal life. In 1973, Hachette published a book on César's jewels, written by James Baldwin and Françoise Giroud. The authors were well aware of the organic nature of the procedure, its revolutionary aspect: while the traditional jewelry made by artists consists merely of small preliminary models or reproductions of original designs to be executed by goldsmiths, César controls the process of total compression from start to finish. His jewelry has the structural monumentality of his large *Compressions*—it is true sculpture, but on a small scale.

Exhibitions

1954

"Animaux en ferraille," One-man show, Galerie Lucien Durand, Paris.

1955

Galerie Rive Droite, Paris (with Appel). – Salon de Mai, Paris.

1956

Venice Biennale. – Galerie Rive Droite, Paris (with Burri).

1957

"Insectes et Nus en ferraille," São Paulo Bienal. – Carrara Biennale, Italy, first prize for foreign participation. – "Bronzetto," International exhibition, Padua. – International exhibition, Galerie Claude Bernard, Paris. – One-man show, Galerie Creuzevault, Paris. – One-man show, The Hanover Gallery, London.

1958

Salon de Mai, Paris. – Sculpture Biennale, Middelheim Park, Antwerp. – Brussels World's Fair, French Pavilion, silver medal. – International sculpture exhibition, Galerie Claude Bernard, Paris. – Carnegie International, Pittsburgh, third prize.

1959

One-man show, Galerie Claude Bernard, Paris. – Salon de Mai, Paris. – "Arte Trivente," Padua. – International sculpture exhibition, Galerie Claude Bernard, Paris. – Documenta II, Kassel. – "New Images of Man," The Museum of Modern Art, New York.

1959–60

"European Art Today" (thirty-five sculptors and painters), traveling exhibition organized by The Minneapolis Institute of Arts.

1960

"Rotterdamsche Kunstkring," Rotterdam. – "Cent Sculpteurs de Daumier à nos jours," Musée d'Art et d'Industrie, Saint-Étienne, France. – "Sculpture contemporaine," Musée Cantini, Marseilles. –

One-man show, The Hanover Gallery, London. – Avant-garde festival, American Pavilion, Porte de Versailles, Paris. – "Petit Bal de têtes," Galerie des Mages, Vence, France. – Salon de Mai, Paris (Automobile *Compressions*).

1961

One-man show, Saidenberg Gallery, New York. – "The Art of Assemblage," The Museum of Modern Art, New York. – "Mechanism and Organism," New School Art Center, New York. – "Jewels 1890–1961," Victoria and Albert Museum, London. – "A 40º au-dessus de Dada," Galerie "J," Paris. – Festival of New Realism, Nice. – Seattle World's Fair. – One-man show, Galleria Apollinaire, Milan (drawings). – "Reliefs," Galerie du XXᵉ Siècle, Paris. – "Mostra Internazionale di Scultura," Galleria Toninelli, Milan.

1962

"Antagonismes II: L'Objet," Musée des Arts Décoratifs, Paris. – "The Art of Assemblage," Dallas and San Francisco.

1963

"Trois sculpteurs: César, Roël d'Haese, Ipoustéguy," Galerie Claude Bernard, Paris. – Second Festival of New Realism, Munich.

1964

Sculpture exhibition, Abbaye de Royaumont, France. – "Figuration et Défiguration," Ghent. – Documenta III, Kassel. – "Painting and Sculpture of a Decade, 54–64," The Tate Gallery, London.

1965

São Paulo Bienal (drawings). – "Open-air Sculptures," Keukenhof Park, Lisse, The Netherlands. – Tokyo Biennale. – "Sculpture et peinture objet," Galerie Creuzevault, Paris. – "Contemporary Graphic Art in France," traveling exhibition in Germany. – "Trois Sculpteurs: César, Roël d'Haese, Tinguely," Musée des Arts Décoratifs, Paris. – "Jeux, sports, jeunesse," Musée Rodin, Paris. – Palais de la Méditerranée, Nice. – "Groupe 1965," Musée d'Art Moderne de la Ville de Paris. – Included in "La Main," Galerie Claude Bernard, Paris (exhibited *Le Pouce*).

1966

Salon de Mai, Musée d'Art Moderne de la Ville de Paris. – One-man show, Stedelijk Museum, Amsterdam, and Wilhelm-Lehmbruck-Museum der Stadt Duisburg, Germany. – One-man show, Galerie Madoura, Cannes. – One-man show, Galleria Il Fante di Spade, Rome. – One-man show, Galatea Galleria d'Arte, Turin. – "Climat 66," Musée de Peinture et de Sculpture, Grenoble. – "Sonsbeek '66," Gemeentemuseum, Arnhem, The Netherlands. – Zonnehof Cultural Center, Amersfoort, The Netherlands (drawings). – Retrospective, Musée Cantini, Marseilles.

1967

"Expansion," Salon de Mai, Paris. – São Paulo Bienal (prize refused). – Group exhibition, Musée de Peinture et de Sculpture, Grenoble. – Expo '67, French Pavilion, Montreal. – Carnegie International, Pittsburgh. – Sculpture exhibition, The Solomon R. Guggenheim Museum, New York. – International exhibition of drawings, Kunsthalle, Darmstadt, Germany. – "Campo Vitale," Palazzo Grassi, Venice. – "Sculpture: A Generation of Innovation," The Art Institute of Chicago. – "Superlund," Lunds Konsthall, Lund, Sweden. – "Tres Escultores," Galería Juana Mordo, Madrid. – "Table d'orientation pour une sculpture d'aujourd'hui," Galerie Creuzevault, Paris. – *Expansions* created in public, Munich; Lund, Sweden; São Paulo; Rio de Janeiro; Montevideo.

1968

One-man show, Galerie Burén, Stockholm. – Exhibition, Göteborgs Konstmuseum, Göteborg, Sweden. – "Assises du siège contemporain," Musée des Arts Décoratifs, Paris. – Group exhibition, Musée de Peinture et de Sculpture, Grenoble. – "Le Décor quotidien de la vie en 1968," Musée Galliera, Paris. – "Images of Man," Kunsthalle, Darmstadt, Germany. – Documenta 4, Kassel. – Milan Triennale. – One-man show, Centre Culturel de Toulouse, France. – *Expansions* created in public, London (The Tate Gallery); Saint-Paul-de-Vence (Fondation Maeght); Göteborg; Brussels (Palais des Beaux-Arts); Ghent (Museum voor Schone Kunsten); Rome (Galleria Nazionale d'Arte Moderna); Paris (Galerie Mathias Fels).

1969

"César chez Daum," Musée des Arts Décoratifs, Paris. – "Compressions," Galerie Mathias Fels, Paris. – One-man show, Pinx Oy Art Gallery, Helsinki. – "Arts 69," Kunstmuseum Athenaeum, Helsinki. – Inaugural exhibition of the Hakone Open-Air Museum, Tokyo. – "Autoportrait," Galerie Creuzevault, Paris. – "Boîtes," Galerie Givaudan, Paris. – *Expansions* created in public, Galleria del Deposito, Genoa.

1970

"Le Peintre Photographié," Musée des Arts Décoratifs, Paris. – "Figuren Gestalten Personen," Kunstverein, Frankfort. – "Depuis Rodin," Musée de Saint-Germain-en-Laye, France. – Group exhibition, Centre Culturel de Toulouse, France. – "Trois Sculpteurs: César, Pavlos, Miralda," Galerie Argos, Nantes, France. – "Bronzetto," Museo Español de Arte Contemporáneo, Madrid. – Scenery for the Ballet Théâtre Contemporain, Maisons de la Culture d'Amiens, Grenoble, Reims, and Rennes, France. – "César, Plastiques," Centre National d'Art Contemporain, Paris. – "Formes libres," Galerie Creuzevault, Paris, and Galleria del Naviglio, Milan. – "Compressions," Galleria del Leone, Venice, and Galleria Schwarz, Milan. – "Cristal," Galerie Rive Gauche, Brussels. – "Le Nouveau Réalisme," festival commemorating the tenth anniversary of New Realism, Milan. *Expansion* created in public, Galleria Vittorio Emanuele II. – "César, Farhi, Arman," Galerie Soissons, Nice. – "Sculptures en acier," Hôtel Intercontinental, Paris.

1971

"Compressions," Galerie Rive Gauche, Brussels. – "Plastiques," Palais des Beaux-Arts, Brussels; Sonja Henie–Niels Onstad Foundation, Oslo; Kunsthalle, Hamburg; and Maison de la Culture, Rennes, France. – Retrospective, Galerie Municipale A.-M. Douet, Montreuil, France. – Galleria Il Centro, Naples. – "Aspects of the Informal," Museo Municipale, Bari, and Galleria Rotonda della Besana, Milan. – "Métamorphose de l'Objet," Palais des Beaux-Arts, Brussels (also Rotterdam, Berlin, Milan). – Biennale de Sculpture, Musée Rodin, Paris. – "Objets et Bijoux compressés," Galerie Semiha Huber, Zurich. – "César sculpteur," Galerie Creuzevault, Paris. – Memorial to the Repatriated, City of Marseilles. – "Sculptures en couleurs," Musée Rodin, Paris. – "Sculptures en plein air," Parc Floral, Vincennes, France. – EAT Art Galerie, Düsseldorf. – "Bijoux," Morabito, Paris. – ROSC '71, Dublin.

1972

"César '72," Musée Cantini, Marseilles. – "Motos," Galerie Mathias Fels, Paris. – "Compressions acryliques," Galerie Lucien Durand, Paris, and Galerie Fred Lanzenberg, Brussels. – "César à Nice," Galerie des Ponchettes, Nice. – "12 Ans d'art contemporain," Expo '72, Grand Palais, Paris. – 100 recent acquisitions, Musée Cantini, Marseilles.

1973

"Compressions acryliques," Théâtre Municipal, Angers, France. – Retrospective, Centre Culturel de Romainville, France. – "Tête à Têtes," Galerie Creuzevault, Paris, and Galerie Semiha Huber, Zurich. – "César, Arles 73," Cloister of Saint-Trophime, Arles. – Contemporary French Art, Edinburgh Festival Society. – "Bronze, Silver and Gold," Alwin Gallery, London. – "Le Portrait," Galeries La Hune, Lacloche, and Bama, Paris. – "Mit Kunst Leben," Kunstverein, Stuttgart. – "Compressions d'or et d'orfèvrerie," Cartier, New York. – "Visage 73," Centre Culturel de Chauny, France. – "Forum de l'Art graphique," Centre d'Art et de Culture, Ghent. – "Masters of Modern Sculpture," Gallery Seibu, Tokyo.

1974

"Jewelry as Sculpture as Jewelry," Institute of Contemporary Art, Boston. – Retrospective, Galleria Rotonda della Besana, Milan. – "Dix Artistes des années soixante," Galerie Mony Calatchi, Paris. – Included in "Étude pour une maison existentielle," exhibition of the work of architect Ico Parisi, Galerie Saint-Germain, Paris. – "Compressions 1962–1972," Galleria d'Arte Il Fauno II, Turin. – Included in "L'Homme et son Empreinte," Château de Sainte-Suzanne, France. – Included in "L'Art du verre," Brussels.

1976 (in preparation)

Retrospective organized by the museums of Geneva and Grenoble, to travel throughout Europe.

Selected Bibliography

Abadie, Daniel. "César et commentaires," *Galerie des Arts*, October, 1969. ● "César et la révolution du matériau," *Études*, June, 1970.
Allemandi, Umberto. "Ave César" (interview), *Bolaffiarte*, No. 34, November, 1973.
"À propos de 'Die grosse Schau von Basel,'" *Magazin Kunst*, No. 51, 1973.
"À propos d'Eurodomus," *Domus*, No. 488, 1970.
"À propos du Salon de Mai," *La Tribune de Lausanne*, 8 May 1968.
"L'Art du cristal," *Galerie des Arts*, No. 88, 1969.
Ashbery, John. "Paris, capitale de la sculpture," *Review Adam*, June, 1964.
Audouin, Jean. "César, des Compressions aux expansions: le sens inné de la matière," *Plastiques-Bâtiment*, October, 1968.
"The Automobile and Art," *General Motors World*, June–July, 1964.
Azcoaga, Enrique. "El Radicalismo expresivo de César, Ipoustéguy y Roël d'Haese," *Blanco y Negro*, 9 December 1967.

Baldwin, James. *César, Compression d'or*. Preface by Françoise Giroud. Paris: Hachette, 1973.
Bernier, Rosamond. "Obsession à Nash House," *L'Œil*, May, 1968.
"Bijoux par César et Arman," *Plaisir de France*, Christmas, 1971.
"Bilan d'une année," *Galerie des Arts*, 1 January 1970.
Boissieu, Jean. "César sous ses masques," *Le Provençal*, 1 April 1973.
Bonnetain, Anne. "L'Amérique et César," *Le Club du Livre américain*, No. 2, 1961.
Bosquet, Alain. "César," *XXe Siècle*, 8 January 1957, p. 70. ● "César: Instantanés," *Combat*, 18 June 1963.
Boudaille, Georges. "Conversation autour d'un pouce avec César," *Les Lettres Françaises*, 30 December 1965.

Cabanne, Pierre. "César," *Lectures pour tous*, May, 1971. ● ed. *César par César*. Paris: Éditions Denoël, 1971. ● and Restany, Pierre. *L'Avant-garde*. Paris: Éditions A. Balland, 1970.
"César," *Alpha Encyclopédie*, 23 October 1968.
"César," *Art International*, May, 1973.
"César," *Brussels Times*, 7 May 1970.
"César," *Centre Culturel, Ville de Toulouse, Bulletin*, November–December, 1968.
"César," *Die Welt*, No. 104, 4 May 1971.
"César," *Gaceta del Arte Madrid*, 30 April 1973.
"César," *Les Muses*, No. 68, 1969.
"César at Nancy," *Art and Artist*, November, 1969.
"César au CNAC," *Vogue*, June–July, 1970.
"César aux Beaux-Arts," *Elle*, No. 1328, May, 1971.
"César chez Daum" (interview), preface to catalogue of exhibition "César–Cristal Daum," Musée des Arts Décoratifs, Paris, 1969.
"César en pleine expansion," *L'Art Vivant*, No. 1 bis, March–April, 1969.
"César en tête-à-tête," *Art-Presse*, No. 4, May, 1973.
"César, la main à la pâte," *Les Lettres Françaises*, 1 October 1969.
"César o el asombro ante la vida," *Triunfo*, 22 February 1969.
"César: Sculture e disegni," *Domus*, September, 1962, p. 36.
"César se comprime y expande," *Analysis*, 29 April 1968.

"César se donne en pâture," *Combat*, 2 April 1973.
"César 'Tête à Têtes,'" *Domus*, No. 522, May, 1973.
"César the Current King of Scrap Metal," *The Times* (London), 10 October 1960.
"C'est avec ça que tu es devenu célèbre," *Paris-Match*, No. 916, 1966.
Chevalier, Denys. *Dictionnaire de la sculpture moderne*. Paris, 1960, p. 52.
"Chicago's Connoisseurs," *Time*, 29 March 1968.
Cogniat, Raymond. "César, moderne Vulcain," *Prisme des Arts*, 7 December 1956. ● "Quand César met la main à la pâte," *Le Figaro* (Paris), 10 March 1973. ● "Trois Générations de sculpteurs," *Le Figaro* (Paris), 21 May 1959.
Conil Lacoste, M. "César en bronze et en brioche," *Le Monde* (Paris), 16 March 1973.
Cooper, Douglas. *César*, Vol. 9 in the "Artistes de notre temps" series. Amriswil, Switzerland: Bodensee-Verlag, 1960. ● Introduction to catalogue of exhibition of works by César from 1955 to 1966, Galerie Madoura, Cannes, 1966. ● Preface to catalogue of exhibition "César en Arles," 1973.

Damase, Jacques. "L'Empire de César," *L'Observateur Littéraire*, 21 May 1959.
Descargues, Pierre. "À propos de Documenta," *Les Lettres Françaises*, 10 July 1963. ● "César ou l'école de la casse," *Les Lettres Françaises*, 28 May 1959. ● "Comment César franchit son Rubicon," *La Tribune de Lausanne*, 18 February 1968.
Deschamps, F. "César," *H.*, June, 1971.
"Des Compressions aux expansions," *Le Monde* (Paris), 30 October 1969.
"Des Sandwiches à la tête de César," *L'Aurore*, 14 March 1973.
"Les deux César," *L'Art Vivant*, No. 6, 1969.
"Dix Ans après la Fête," *Combat*, 2 November 1970.
"Duel Raysse-César," *Arts Loisirs*, June, 1967.

Entretien avec Catherine Vallogne," *Les Lettres Françaises*, 12 April 1972.
"Entretien avec César," *Architectes*, November, 1971.
"Entretien avec César, créateur du siège total," *Bureaux d'Aujourd'hui*, September, 1968.
"Environnement, Décoration. Une nouvelle conquête de César: Daum," *L'Officiel de l'Ameublement*, December, 1969.
"The Expanding World of Art," *The Sunday Times* (London), 3 March 1968.
"L'Expansion de César," *Le Figaro* (Paris), 8 May 1968.
"Expansion von César," *Die Kunst*, August, 1970.
"L'Express va plus loin avec César," *L'Express*, 8 November 1971.

"**F**ace à face–Ave César," *Spécial Bruxelles*, 13 May 1970.
"Festival du Nouveau Réalisme à Milan," *Zeit Magazin*, December, 1970.

Gallois, Anne. "César ou l'art mécanisé," *Clubinter*, June–July, 1968.
Gindertael, Roger van. "La Sculpture à Marseille," *XXe Siècle*, June, 1960, p. 100. ● "La Sculpture de César," *Les Beaux-Arts*, 22 May 1959.
Giraudy, Danielle. Preface to catalogue of exhibition "César," Musée Cantini, Marseilles, 1972.
Giroud, Françoise. "L'Air des bijoux," *Figaro Littéraire*, 24 November 1973.

Hagen, Yvonne. "Sculptured Scrap," *New York Herald Tribune*, 20 May 1959.
Hahn, Otto. "César au fournil," *L'Express*, No. 1132, 19 February 1973. ● "César saisi par la matière," *L'Express*, 29 September 1969.
Händler, Gerhard. Introduction to catalogue of César exhibition, Wilhelm-Lehmbruck-Museum der Stadt Duisburg, Germany, 1966.

230

Hunter, Sam. Introduction to catalogue *César: Sculptures 1953–1961*. Saidenberg Gallery, New York, 1961.

"L'Imagination en liberté," *Maison de Marie-Claire*, December, 1970.

"Jacques Daum, où s'arrêtera-t-il?" *Maison de Marie-Claire*, No. 35, January, 1970.
Jaguer, Édouard. "César et l'homme paléontologique," *Les Cahiers du Musée de Poche*, March, 1959. ● "Poétique de la sculpture," *Les Cahiers du Musée de Poche*, 1960.
Jouffroy, Alain. "Qui est César," *Opus International*, No. 17, April, 1970.

Lebel, Robert. "Premier Bilan de l'art actuel (1937–1953)," *Le Soleil Noir, Position*, Nos. 3 and 4, 1953, pp. 269, 278.
Lévêque, J.-J. "Les Matériaux sujets," *Jardin des Arts*, January, 1974.
Limbour, Georges. "César," *Les Lettres Nouvelles*, 20 May 1959.

Mathey, François. Introduction to catalogue of the César exhibition, Stedelijk Museum, Amsterdam, 1966. ● Introduction to catalogue of the César-Roël d'Haese-Tinguely exhibition, Musée des Arts Décoratifs, Paris, June–September, 1965. ● Cooper, Douglas. Prefaces to catalogue of the César exhibition, Musée Cantini, Marseilles, 1966. ● Restany, Pierre. Introductions to catalogue *César*. CNAC, Paris, 1970.
Mattéi, F. "Mais comment s'en débarrasser?" *2000*, January, 1971.
Michel, Jacques. "Le Retour de César," *Le Monde* (Paris), 30 October 1969.
"Le Monde fantastique des sculptures de César," *La Croix*, 10 November 1968.
"Le Moteur à 2 temps qui fait marcher César," *L'Auto-Journal*, 23 September 1971.
"Motos," *L'Express*, 15 September 1971.
Muller, Grégoire. "Der Plastiker César," *Du*, February, 1968.

Pivot, Bernard. "César, le fonceur timide," *Figaro Littéraire*, 20 October 1969.
Pluchart, François. "César passe au rouge," *Combat*, 1 February 1971. ● "C.Q.F.D.," *Combat*, 25 May 1970. ● "Dans les Fers de César perçait déjà le Nouveau Réalisme," *Combat*, 4 November 1971. ● "La Fête de la technologie," *Combat*, 9 December 1968. ● "La Quatrième Révolution de César," *XXe Siècle*, June, 1969, p. 65.
"Le Pouce," *Frankfurter Allgemeine Zeitung*, 12 June 1968.
"Pourquoi j'ai choisi Nice," *L'Express-Méditerranée*, November, 1970.

Ragon, Michel. "César sculpteur de l'âge industriel," *Jardin des Arts*, No. 154, September, 1967, p. 50 (article reprinted in Ragon, Michel. *Vingt-cinq Ans d'art vivant*. Paris, 1969). ● "Le Relief dans l'art contemporain," *Jardin des Arts*, January, 1962, p. 32.
Raillard, Georges. "Visite à César," *L'Arc*, No. 3, 1958.
"Renaissance de l'objet-art depuis 1945," *Du*, September, 1969.
"Les Rencontres de César," *Droit et Liberté*, September, 1970.
Restany, Pierre. "César," *Das Kunstwerk*, 7 January 1962, p. 13. ● "César à la Rotonda della via Besana," *Bolaffiarte*, No. 38, 1974. ● "César en expansion," *Galerie des Arts*, No. 46, July–September, 1967. ● "César: La Poésie pure de la chimie industrielle," *Domus*, No. 462, May, 1968. ● "César Tête à Têtes," *Magazin Kunst*, No. 52, 1974.

● "Die Beseelung des Objektes," *Das Kunstwerk*, July, 1961. ● "Du César tout en cristal," *Domus*, No. 483, February, 1970. ● "Expansion et environnement," introduction to catalogue of exhibition "Le Décor quotidien de la vie en 1968," Musée Galliera, Paris, 1968. ● "Festival du Nouveau Réalisme à Milan," *Domus*, No. 483, February, 1970. ● "Da Parigi: Il Pollice di César," *Domus*, No. 435, February, 1966. ● Introduction to catalogue of exhibition "César: Recent Sculpture," The Hanover Gallery, London, 1960. ● Introduction to catalogue of exhibition "À 40° au-dessus de Dada," Galerie "J," Paris, 1961. ● Introduction to catalogue commemorating the tenth anniversary of New Realism, Milan, 1970. ● "Le Baptême de l'objet," *Ring des Arts*, No. 2, 1961. ● *Le Livre blanc de l'art total*. Milan: Edizioni Apollinaire, April, 1969. ● *Le Livre rouge de la révolution picturale*. Milan: Edizioni Apollinaire, May, 1968. ● "Le Nouveau Réalisme, que faut-il en penser?" Introduction to the second New Realism Festival, Munich, 1963. ● "Le Pouce de César," *Domus*, No. 435, 1965. ● *Le Plastique dans l'Art*. Monaco: Éditions Sauret, 1974. ● "Les Nouveaux Réalistes," preface to the first New Realism Festival, Nice, 1961. ● *Les Nouveaux Réalistes*. Paris: Éditions Planète, 1968. ● "Notre Actuelle Avant-garde," *Planète*, No. 1, October, 1961. ● "Un Nouveau Réalisme en sculpture," *Cimaise*, No. 55, October, 1961. ● "Pour une esthétique prospective," *Domus*, No. 469, 1968. ● Preface to catalogue of exhibition "Tête à Têtes," Galerie Creuzevault, Paris, 1973. ● "Un Tour de Maître," preface to catalogue of exhibition "Compressions," Galerie Mathias Fels, Paris, 1969.
Rey, Jean-Dominique. "César," *ATAC Informations*, No. 4, January, 1967.
Roger-Marx, Claude. "Il faut copier pour être soi-même," *Figaro Littéraire*, 3 March 1969. ● "Les Enfants s'amusent," *Figaro Littéraire*, 11 December 1967.
Russell, John. "César à Londres," *XXe Siècle*, No. 16, May, 1961, p. 84. ● Preface to catalogue of César exhibition, The Hanover Gallery, London, 1957.

Salvy, Claude. "César, de la tôle au cristal," *Les Nouvelles Littéraires*, 9 October 1969.
"Der Schaum und ich," *Der Spiegel*, No. 22, 1971.
Schröder, Thomas. "César: sein Daumen ist grösser als er selbst," *Twen*, August, 1970.
"Le Sculpteur César," *Die Kunst*, August, 1971.
"Le Sculpteur César va se donner en pâture à ses admirateurs," *France-Soir*, 3 March 1973.
"Le Sculpteur se met à compresser des bijoux," *Herald Tribune* (Paris), 16 December 1971.
"Sein pour l'usine Rochas," *Der Spiegel*, 24 February 1969.
Seitz, William C. "Assemblage: Problems and Issues," *Art International*, January, 1962, p. 26.
Selz, Peter, with Statements by the artists. *New Images of Man*. New York, 1959.
Seuphor, Michel. "La Sculpture de ce siècle," *Dictionnaire de la Sculpture moderne*. Neuchâtel, 1959. ● "Le Choix d'un critique," *L'Œil*, January, 1959, p. 24.

Taillandier, Yvon. "Il ne faut pas se plier à la technique," *XXe Siècle*, May–June, 1959, p. 57.
Trier, Eduard. *Figur und Skulptur des XX. Jahrhunderts*. Berlin, 1960, p. 37.

Volboudt, P. "À Chacun sa réalité," *XXe Siècle*, 9 June 1957, p. 32. ● "César: l'Œuvre récent," *XXe Siècle*, No. 25, December, 1963, p. 79.

Waldberg, Patrick. "Rendons à César," *Les Nouvelles Littéraires*, 11 January 1962.

Zegel, Sylvain. "Quand César compresse son passé," *Le Figaro* (Paris), 5 November 1971.

Photograph Credits